THE MILLENIUM DISCOURSES

ETSKO SCHUITEMA

INTENT PUBLISHING

About our logo:
The square in the middle represents The One, from The One come the
two surrounding lines, the 'Outward' and the 'Inward'.
The next four are the 'Sensory' and 'Meaning' aspects of the 'Inward' and
'Outward', and the last eight the 'Celestial' and 'Terrestrial' manifestations
of the previous aspects.

CONTENTS

Acknowledgements:

I am deeply grateful to Tawheda Schuitema, Fayruz Abrahams and Amatullah Armstrong for the many hours spent on polishing what was a very crude text. All the footnotes are theirs and are introduced with their initials.

Etsko Schuitema, *(Shaykh Ebrahim Schuitema)*
March 2009

http://www.zawiaebrahim.co.za   http://www.schuitema.co.za

FOREWORD

I personally feel that Shaykh Ebrahim Schuitema's work is extremely profound and I think that not many people know it's true value. From many aspects his work is of the calibre of a mujaddid. A Mujaddid is a person who presents the Deen of Islam in its real form after removing all that is not deen. This term has its roots in a Hadith wherein the Rasul (s.a.w.s) predicted that every century will have a Mujaddid.

I especially appreciate his articulation of the issues of intent and transactional correctness and their application in professional life. I have yet to see a simpler explanation in contemporary language and logic. He presents intent as a master key that unlocks the door to understanding everything. Secondly, his work is real Dawah (invitation). The target of Dawah is all humanity, not only the Muslims, and I feel that Shaykh Ebrahim's work has this Universal appeal.

Shaykh Sayed Fakhir Hassan Shah.

Authors Introduction

This book is a selection of discourses often referred to as a dars. Within the Darqawi Sufi order a dars is usually delivered by the shaykh or a designated muqaddam (representative) after a session of dhikr (remembrance or invocation), when all concerned are in a deep and quiet state. It is never rehearsed or prepared, it is spontaneous and can be described as the process whereby the shaykh teases out a theme which becomes apparent to him in the few moments of silence that follow the final recitation of the Qur'an after the dhikr.

When one participates in the dhikr circle one becomes connected by and with the other people in the circle. One stops existing as an isolated individual and those who do dhikr together on a regular basis become connected in the unseen.

This connectedness creates the possibility of great openings for everybody concerned. When people sit in the dhikr circle they form a lens that focuses the Divine Light to such an intensity that it dissipates any darkness within and the assumption that they are separate from existence. They become peaceful, undistracted and undisturbed. Their eloquence is in submitting, not in commanding. It is a handing over of control rather than being in charge.

These discourses should therefore not be viewed as a position taken in a debate. They should be viewed as a totality and mulled over in order to taste the state of both the shaykh and the company of fuqara at the time. There are two ways of knowing. The first is by intellectual argument or maintaining a position by quoting reams of text. The other is by experience, by taste, our curiosity is regarding the second.

A further point of interest regarding this particular series of dars is that they were all recorded in 2000 and 2001, which was a very significant time for us all, as it was a time when the combative confrontation between Islam and the West had taken on both global and millenarian proportions.

Therefore there is a theme sitting at the root of all of these discourses, which is the struggle with what it means to be appropriate in these highly polarised times. Fundamentally, the mess that the Islamic Ummah (community) is in at the moment seems to suggest that we are really getting this thing wrong.

Shaykh Ebrahim Schuitema

IQRAA: READING THE TEXT
Discourse 1: 29 September 2000

Bismillahir Rahmanir Rahim

The reason we do dhikr is that it enables us to worship Allah with our mouths, our tongues, limbs, and hearts and with our chests. This worshipping with our whole beings allows us to open a door. The opening of the door is the dhikr itself. The entrance into the court of the King is in the silence that follows the dhikr and in the pauses between the various dhikrs. If, in those few moments of quiet, you sit deliberately still and watch, like a cat before a mouse hole, you are ushered into the presence of the Lord for a personal audience, and it is you who are doing the listening and the hearing.

Our freedom lies in our capability to be still. It is only when we are still that we are in a position to correctly appraise that which Allah is putting in front of us. If you are on the path you must have the capacity to suspend your own agenda and to stop talking to yourself; to silence your inner dialogue. The dhikr delivers us to a place where, for a few moments, this aperture of silence appears. We have a taste of peace.

Peace is not full of something. The more full you are of things, the more disturbed your being is. The noisier your inner dialogue is, the more you ramble on inside your mind about your concerns, your fears, and your hopes, the less peace you have. It is precisely the fact that we are always talking to ourselves about what we would like to have and what we wish to avoid, that we are in a state of agitation, in a place where we have no peace or fulfilment.

As soon as you conceive a desire, the desire itself tells you that you are not fulfilled. If I say; 'Oh, you know, I must have this new car, or I must have that pair of shoes' what I am saying to myself is that I suffer from a state of incompleteness, and thus I experience disturbance, until I achieve that state of having shoes, or that state of having a car. So the person who is most free and expansive is not the one who is imprinting on his being all of these noises about his own inadequacies and desires. He is the one who has learned the very useful skill of not talking to himself and of suspending his inner dialogue.

The capacity to suspend our inner dialogue is the first aspect of our path, because being able to still your own desire creates the conditions where your attention can be appropriately orientated towards the other, toward the person who is in front of you or the situation that confronts you. If you appraise the situation that is in front of you on the basis of what you want from it, on the basis of your own agenda, you create the conditions where the situation has power over you.

If you want something from somebody else, that person's ability to withhold what you want makes you manipulable. They are strong and you are weak. When you appraise the person or situation in front of you with your own agenda, with what you want to get and with your desires, you create the condition where the situation that is in front of you determines you. It has power over you.

Then of course there is another possibility: You do not deal with the situation in front of you on the basis of what you want to get from it, but you deal with it on the basis of what you should be contributing to it. What you should be giving. When you respond on that basis, you are immediately responding on the basis of something which is bigger than yourself. The person who defines the outcome of events is the person who deals with the situation from the basis of what he should be putting in, on the basis of what he is willing to lose. In other words, what he is willing to give away. The more unconditional you are about that, the more you change the outcome of events. In its extremity, you will see this in the case of the person who is utterly unconditional, and is willing to lose everything.

The man who is willing to die right now for what he believes is right, cannot be manipulated by anyone. You cannot manipulate a kamikaze pilot. In other words, the more unconditional you are about what you need to contribute, put in, or give to any situation, the more you grow out of that situation. You transcend the situation. It no longer defines you, you define it. You become bigger than it, you change. Whereas if you confront the situation on the basis of what you want to get from it, it defines you and you get stuck.

Another way of looking at this is that every moment that Allah presents to you has something due to it from you. Acting consistently with what is due we call courtesy. If you do not respond with the appropriate courtesy then the moment denies to you the message it has for you, the learning it has for you. You first have to hand over the toll to the Gatekeeper before you can continue on the journey. The toll which is asked of you in the moment is always a pittance. When you pay what Allah asks of you in the moment, then by His Rahmat, He will give you many multiples more than you could ever have imagined. This is the extraordinary nature of His design. He gives incalculably more than you can give. How many times did the Rasul (s.a.w.s.) refer to the blessing of Allah for good actions to be in seemingly unreasonable multiples; tens, hundreds, thousands and so on. This is what this means.

Any good deed is rewarded beyond measure. In other words, when you deal with the situation in front of you on the basis of what Allah wants from you, what you should be contributing, you are increased and you grow. You change beyond measure. Whereas, if you confront the situation on the basis of your desires, what you want to get out of the situation, then you are frozen there. You are delayed at the gate.

When you act on your own agenda you are attempting to manage your affair, and we know that when we wish to manage our own affair Allah lets us get on with it. He leaves us to manage our own affair. The person who wants to manage his own affair is left to manage his own affair. This managing of your own affair is closing off the portals to the multiple effects of Allah's Baraka. So at best you can only have what you thought you would have. What an anticlimax. What surprise is there in getting what you knew was your due?

At best, the outcome of managing your affair is mediocrity and boredom. At worst, it is a catastrophic mess because it is not possible for you to manage your own affair. Your affair, by definition, is infinitely more complex than your capacity to be in charge of it. Whether you recognize it or not, life only continues, moment by moment, because of a superordinate genius which you cannot remotely begin to fathom, let alone manage.

Here is another theme we have spoken about many times. You cannot even account for the metabolic processes that make your finger work. Now you want to account for your life. What presumption! Which means to say that the more you try to be in charge and work out what it is that you want and make the universe fit your desires, the more you go astray and lose control.

The attempt to control the fundamentally uncontrollable is what one could call lack of control. It is losing it utterly, to the point of collapse. All control is fundamentally concerned with making sure things go our way. It is about defining the future. However, we are all going to die. Our future is not definite, it is indefinite. It is fundamentally uncontrollable. It does not matter how you build the wall, how secure you build the structure of your security, death will find you there. It will seek you out.

Which is to say, the whole process of our growth as human beings is based on a very simple dynamic, and that simple dynamic is that we give every situation that confronts us its due. Giving every moment its due is only possible when we see it for what it is, when we give it the attention due to it. In other words, when Allah confronts us with something, we do not immediately try to work out what we can get out of the situation, rather, we give the situation it's due attention. We suspend our agenda to see what really is required by the other. We silence our own inner chatter so that we can properly appraise the situation and are in a position to see what we are being called on to give.

If you ever had a conversation with someone, and in the course of the conversation you were trying to say something to the other person but that person answered you back before you finished speaking, you would not have felt heard. This means to say that for this person to give attention, they have to shut up. They have to stop giving attention to their own agenda because only then can they give attention to yours. They have got to stop talking to themselves. This means that you cannot give any situation that you are in the attention that it requires unless you stop talking to yourself about the situation. Unless you have this capacity to shut up.

We are taught that this path is about being still. This is the necessary precursor to seeing things as they are and giving everything its due. Seeing things as they are is based on the ability to suspend one's own agenda in any given situation. Giving the other their due is based on enacting the rule of courtesy that is operative in that situation. The situation has a requirement, which is the courtesy appropriate to it. If you act consistently with that courtesy, you change. If you act against that courtesy, then you do not go out of the situation, the situation diminishes you.

The five dhikrs of our wird are specifically designed to cultivate in us this skill of silencing our inner dialogue so that we can see everything for what it is and therefore be in the position to give everything its due. These are the five dhikrs; *"Astaghfirrullah"*, *"Masha'Allah"*, *"Subhaan'Allah"*, *"Hasbunallah wa ni'mal Wakil"* and *"Allah"*. Now why is that the case?

Our inner dialogue is sustained by hopes and fears, and because this is the case it is biographically based. Let's say I had an obsessive desire for a red Porsche. The first question to ask here is why a red Porsche and not a brown mule? Why is a red Porsche such a desirable thing for me? This has to be that I have learned in the past that to have a red Porsche is a desirable thing. If I had no idea what a car was, let alone what a red Porsche was I would probably be terrified the first time I saw one.

This means I can only want what I know of, and what I know of has to have been presented to me at least once before because otherwise I would not recognize it. This means to say that all my desires are historically and biographically based. They are based on what I have learned in the past. Each desire is a definition of a lack. The lack of the thing makes having the thing desirable. My lack is about my inadequacy, my neediness and my brokenness.

Shutting up your agenda means that you have the capacity to silence your past. You can shut down your biography. Astaghfirrullah is about shutting down one's biography. It is a very poor and shallow understanding of Istighfaar to say it is about forgiveness, because it is deeper than forgiveness. The word means literally 'to cover'. So what do you say to Allah when you say *"please cover me"*?

You say, not forgive me, you say, cover where I have been so that I can go elsewhere. Cover the known. Cover my presumption. Cover my assumptions of what I think, my assumption of what I want to pursue, so that I can be available to what You want for me. I know that what You want for me is infinitely better than what I can ever want for myself.

"Julle maak planne, maar Allah maak planne vir julle", (We plan, but Allah is the Best of Planners). There is always something foreboding in that statement, but you must understand that the plans He is making for you are better for you than your plan. Every single parameter will be better. The best thing you can wish for yourself, Allah has a hundred times better than that for you. However, you must do what is required of you. Do not make your agenda the getting part of your life. Make your agenda the contributing part of your life, what you should be giving. This is what istighfaar is about. Istighfaar is about the capacity to shut down your agenda by covering yourself.

Forget this knot of historically based presumption that you think you are. Make it irrelevant, just forget it. Don't wash it away, don't forgive it, just forget it, just cover it. This delivers you to a remarkable state, the capacity to do true tauba, true repentance. Repentance does not confirm your brokenness, it makes it irrelevant. Your brokenness and your neediness are the same thing. When you cover who you assume you are, you are delivered to a place where you are looking at the moment that confronts you without wanting anything from it, because you have stopped wanting. You have shut up the inner recording of lack. You have forgotten about red Porsches and green Porsches. They are irrelevant. You are looking at it with an innocent eye, and when you look at the situation with an innocent eye, you cannot but recognize that the moment that confronts you has come directly from Allah. It is by His decree, Masha'Allah. (As Allah wills)

The first command to the Rasul (s.a.w.s.) was *"Iqra'a"*, which means 'read', and it suggests to not just read the book, it also suggests that the whole of existence is a text. We know that Shaykh Muhammad Ibn al Habib, says; *"All created things are meanings set up as images"*. You are walking through a text. It is a book. It is all meanings, every moment that confronts you is the next page of that book and this is a remarkable book. One that you want to read because this book is not a general book.

This book is a letter that is being addressed by the Creator of all, to you personally.

The moment that stands in front of you is the next paragraph of that text. What is required of us is to read the paragraph and to read it well, because the letter also functions as a kind of treasure map. It is both a very personal, intimate love letter and a treasure map. If you read a treasure map properly, then it indicates what the next steps are, and if you follow those steps you are closer yet again to the treasure. This treasure is the treasure of all treasures. It is the essence of all delight, all joy. What else is there to say to this but *"Subhaan'Allah?"* (Glory be to Allah)

So the letter that Allah writes to you is a letter concerning a treasure map, concerning a journey, and you have got to read the instructions very carefully. The instructions are in the moment that sits in front of you. The moment is a paragraph in the letter that contains the next instruction, and what does that instruction tell you?

Act consistently with the courtesy of the situation. Smile at the child, move the stone out of the road, lift something up to the traveller on his horse, make tea for the guests, whatever. You do that.

As a host you do not look at the guest from the point of view of what you can get out of him. As a guest you do not look at the host from the point of view of how you can make him convenient to you. Even as a guest there is a certain courtesy that you afford the host. That is what the situation requires. So if you are in a situation and the next paragraph says that you should behave as the proper guest, without the intention of getting something out of your host, and you do that, then the next thing happens, then there is change that follows, and that change always delivers you to a better place than what you could have imagined.

This does not mean to suggest that you will always recognize that where you have been brought to is a superior place to where you were. Very often we do not like where we are at in the immediacy of it. However, with a little hindsight and the intent to see the blessing in the situation, the benefit of where Allah has placed us soon becomes apparent.

When you understand that the moment in front of you is decreed by Allah: *"Masha'Allah."* You then act accordingly and you take these next ten steps and you are transported to a place where: Subhaan'Allah, is that not amazing! Look, He has brought me to the place which is already a treasure! When you act with innocence on the basis of what Allah wants from you in any given situation, He will immediately place you in a better situation.

You then realize that indeed He has better in store for you than yourself. You recognize that Allah is enough for you and that you need no other protector: *"Hasbunallah wa ni'mal wakil."* This is His promise to us. So you arrive at the next place or in a next moment, only being able to praise and glorify Allah. This is what it means to act fisabilillah. If you do that, unconditionally in the moment you are in, then in the next moment you have the garden.

As you arrive at a point, the only thing that remains is to be perpetually surprised, where you cannot even say; *"Astaghfirrullah, Masha'Allah, Subahana'Allah, Hasbunallah wa ni'mal wakil"* because the whole process, the journey is going so fast. It is like a skyrocket taking off: *"Allah, Allah, Allah!"* Look! Moment after moment, amazing grandeur, majesty, mercy, you see more and more of His attributes in front of you, demonstrated in front of you, in ways that keep on surprising you, you eventually have nowhere to turn. You are like a madman, everywhere you turn is His Significance. There is none but Him. *"La illaha il Allah."*

Our normal lives are so mediocre and humdrum, that maybe we will be surprised once a week. Amazing! This is so because we are walking through life with blinkers on our eyes, because we are not looking out, we are looking in. We are not listening at all. It is like this man who is about to be knocked down by a car, but he is so furious with his wife that he does not notice the car. What is going on in his mind is this argument with this phantom woman in his head. His attention is certainly not on the road he is about to cross. Meanwhile, she is in the house, doing the same thing. She is about to chop her finger off with a knife because she is having the last word to him in her mind.

We are not present because of our own inner dialogue. That inner dialogue creates the conditions that cause us to miss the surprise that is in the moment; like the car that is about to take that fellow out.

So the further you progress on the journey, the more you are able to suspend your inner dialogue, your own agenda, the more surprised you will become. Surprise, wonder and amazement. Being ravished, bereft, breath taken and amazed. This state is not a state for once in a while or once in a lifetime, or once a week, it is every moment's state. It is the pinnacle of human experience.

It is the ecstasy we have been made for. If you do not experience this state in every moment you have anaesthetized yourself.

_____

May Allah grant us success on the path.
May He grant us nearness to Him.

May He grant us annihilation in Him.
Allah, grant peace and blessings on our blessed Nabi (s.a.w.s.)

Al Hamdulillah.

———

1: - The first word of the Qur'anic revelation: "Read (iqra'a): In the name of thy Lord who createth. Createth man from a clot." [96:1-2]. Familiarity with the glossary will be essential to understand this text.

PATIENCE AND GRATITUDE: SEEING THINGS AS THEY ARE
Discourse 2: Undated

Bismillahir Rahmanir Rahim:

Shaykh Muhammad Ibn al Habib writes in one of the qasidas of his diwan that he asked his heart why it is that he cannot see his Lord, since his Lord was inescapable and ever present. The answer came that he could not see Him because of veils. We do not see things as they are because of successive layers of veiling which filter out the light and the effulgence of existence as it is.

It is literally like being in a room with a metre thick set of veils, or of curtains in front of the window. Every curtain blocks out a little bit of the light, so that by the time that the light gets to the last curtain there is no light left and you are in darkness, you do not see the light.

That is exactly as it is with our existence. We do not see things as they are because we are veiled from them. We have filters that block out the radiance of existence and leave us in a place of exile and a place of darkness where we assume that there is no light. We are positive that there must be light, but this is an intellectual position. It is not based on witnessing and the result of that is that we might be able to quote reams of hadith or recite the entire Qur'an but there is no luminosity, there is no light as a result. In fact, very often our deen itself becomes a veiling.

It becomes part of the filters which trap the effulgence instead of being part of our stripping away and becoming naked in the light of Allah Subhanahu wa ta'ala. Sometimes the most intelligent people who have studied the most are the furthest away. Shaykh Abdul Qadir said on numerous occasions that you will find a lot of very stupid people in paradise because they are not trying to work it out.

Every time that you try and work it out, you set another veil. Your working it out is a veiling. There is a difference between seeing the thing and thinking about what you see, or interpreting, or making an assertion, or making an assumption about what you see. These are not the same things.

In this matter of nearness to Allah the majdhoob witnesses more, sees more and is in a more direct contact with the Light than the man who is learned and who spent his years studying books. In terms of matters as they actually are the one who is mad in Allah is fundamentally more successful at his existence than the person who has turned his existence into a big intellectual exercise.

Why do we exist? Why has Allah made us? He has made us to witness Him. It is like this extraordinary story I once heard about certain Vedic rishis who chant the Vedas. These are people who can go into the finest detail in Sanskrit about the deepest possibility of inner witnessing and yet they themselves have not tasted a minute of these states and further more they have no desire to do so. So they can say that enlightenment is blah, blah, blah but they do not know what it is on the basis of first hand experience. They talk about it. So the code that is supposed to bring them to enlightenment is yet another veil that blocks them from it. Enlightenment is letting the Light in and escaping the darkness of your inner niche. That is what enlightenment means. It means being flooded by a light so intense, so bright, that there is no room left for you.

These veils that we set up between existence and ourselves are principally veils defined in language. They are all assumptions about how things are. These assumptions are more often than not, a set of value judgments. This is better than that, this is higher than that, this is more significant than that, and this is tastier than that. So we set up a whole series of attractions and repulsions.

Every one of these judgments sets up a pattern of limitation and restriction. Furthermore, every judgment of the world delineates the structure of the self. My judgment of the other says much more about me and my likes and dislikes than it does about the other. Every time I judge something, I am drawing a line of my discontinuity. I am saying to myself *"I am here, I am not there"*. Every one of these statements therefore is a statement of limitation. It is as if I choose restriction where I could have expansiveness.

Read for restriction darkness, read for expansiveness light. My internal diatribe quite literally keeps me in the dark.

Every definition is separating because it is based on delineating, discriminating and distinguishing. If you say that this is a dog and you have an idea of what 'dogness' means, it implies that you somehow take the individual and reduce it to a generalization. So that you do not see the thing as it is. You are looking at your assumption of what dogs look like, of what dogs are.

You see this very often with people. We have for example the popular assumption among African and Asian Muslims that all Americans are bad. Amazing that one can assert this. There are some 230 million of these people; chances are that there might be a good one. The problem is that because your assumption of the world is that all Americans are bad, you subsequently treat every American as bad. So he behaves to you in a bad way because you set it up that way. You meet this fellow and you hear an American accent and so you are rude to him and he is obviously rude back to you because you have been rude to him and then you say *"You see, all Americans are rude."*

We set up the world on the basis of our assumptions. Those of us who come from the history of the Murabitun will remember how very good we were at this. We had such a tightly defined universe that the only worthwhile human beings for a Murabit to know were other Murabitun, the rest were cannon fodder. This one prays like this, clutching his stomach and it becomes a big source of mirth. This one has this idea and that one has that idea, and they are all wrong because it is not our idea. The Jews are this and the Christians are like that. They are all in collusion. Eventually you live in a world that is so small it is just this tiny patch and everything else is filtered out.

So you are sitting in a train and there is a man next to you and for all that you know he is a great poet, but all you are seeing is this little piece of cloth on his head and that is what you respond to, not the person. **2.** So we limit our own experience, we define our universe to something that has become tight and restricted and then we complain about being alienated.

Then we say; 'Oh life is so lonely, look at how miserable it all is, just look at it; the world is in such a mess.' It is not in a mess.

There is far more good about it than bad. If there was not far more good about it than bad it would not exist. It would not be here. For a thing to exist there has to be more life in it than death, otherwise it could not be alive. By definition your life and who you are has to have more affirmation than negation. If there were more negation than affirmation you would not even be a pile of bones. You would not be, but you are.

You see, all of our definitions are based on negation. This is like this, not like that. Now there is a place for this negation, but it is the baby talk of being human. When you are on this path, the path of liberation, you are on the path of deliberately stripping away the veils. Stripping away the veils means stripping away your assumptions and your presumptions. It means learning to apprehend things without finding fault, without defining it, without this constant internal dialogue that we have with ourselves.

I sometimes wonder why anybody needs to watch television. Just look at what goes on in your own head in one afternoon. Just recall what you thought about during the last hour. Don't be surprised if you find what you see appalling. This is because we are mostly not conscious of how we actually function. We somnambulate, sleepwalk, wandering around in a dream of our own making. This causes the kind of distraction where, for example, I walk into the wall or I bump into somebody and I say; *"Oh I am sorry, I was not looking"*.

Why was I not looking? Because my attention was not on what was going on around me, my attention was on what was going on in my head. It is almost as if my eyes were oriented to the movie playing at the back of my skull. There is no way that the movie at the back of my skull can be anything like the reality that is in front of me. What is at the back of my skull is imagination. It is presumption. It is noise. It is ugly by definition. Shaykh Muhammad Ibn al Habib says; 'find nothing attractive about the self, view everything about it as ugly'. As soon as you are entranced with anything about the self, say; astaghfirrullah it is ugly. That is the root of ugliness. The root of ugliness is the attention of a person twisted in on itself to find the self significant and interesting. That is darkness.

I do not let the Light in because my attention is orientated towards itself. This inner noise is made up of presumptions that we have; the veils that we keep putting up. This constitutes the blocking out, the veiling. So the path that we are on is the successive stripping away of the veils. This stripping away means changing your habits. Find yourself three Jewish friends. That is changing your habit. Changing your habit is not having tea today because you had coffee yesterday. Who are you fooling? It means to put yourself on the spot that you sweat. It means finding your most pernicious presumption and deliberately acting contrary to it. That is changing your habit.

You know, there will come a day when we will be standing in front of Allah and He will say; 'I gave you every opportunity to be astonished every minute of your life because I have moment by moment presented you either with a name of Majesty or with a name of Beauty. So why did you not experience moment by moment amazement at Me and at My wonderful works? Because you could not see what I was putting in front of you because you were too busy watching the video in your head and imposing your assumptions on the world. You said that this person in front of you comes from this background and that he by definition can have nothing to tell you. He must shut-up and listen to you because you are the significant one in this transaction.'

The secret to making a success is to dismiss nothing. It is to assume that what you are presented with in every moment has a secret for you. That is exactly what it is. That is exactly how Allah works, and when you apply this principle your life becomes magical. It does not matter where you are - you can be in the street or in prison. When you wake up in the morning say: 'there is a secret hidden for me in this moment', and you will find the wonder in that moment. Every moment can be like that, but we chase careers and we chase money and we chase all sorts of fundamentally worthless things. **3.**

You miss that coffee that you were drinking that had the ability to fill your being with the most wonderful fragrance, because you were not there. Your attention was not on this smooth ambrosia in your mouth; it was already in the traffic on the way to work. We are like the village of the walking dead. We do not have our lives. We only have our assumptions and our inner dialogue of concerns with the future and the past, everything other than the moment we are in.

When Allah visits us with His names of Majesty He smashes our presumptions and says to us 'Shut-up now'. When Allah changes our lives, turns them upside-down, we sit in a corner and we feel sorry for ourselves. That is the time when we should say; *"Al Hamdulillah, Subhaanallah."* That is when you see Allah's Hand. That is when the openings take place and the veils get lifted. Examine your past. Examine the major times of change in your life and ask yourself whether it was not precipitated by a staggering crisis? You are lying to yourself if that is not the case. Every single time that you really had a significant shift as a human being it was because Allah visited upon you His names of Majesty, His names of confrontation. 'This is who you are,' and then you were shocked into silence. For a moment you stopped jabbering away to yourself about how clever you are and how everything is under your thumb.

All the practices of the deen and particularly that of the dhikr have one aim in mind and that aim is to silence the inner dialogue. The silencing of the inner dialogue has the effect of stripping away the veils. As you sit in dhikr, immediately after the dhikr, if nothing else, you will have experienced quietness. You cannot think much because you have just blasted your brain with oxygen. It is not possible to think. In that moment when you are not thinking, just observe. Watch your breath, watch as the things come into your being and that is when you start discovering the secrets. That is when the radiance starts to come through. Every time that you shutdown your inner-dialogue you strip away a few of those veils. If you do it regularly over a period of time, if you do it with commitment, then this removing of the veils becomes a consistent experience. Then finally there are very few veils. Then there is luminosity all the time. Then the 'niche' in your heart is flooded with a Light that never leaves you. You are pickled in a delight that stays constant irrespective of what the world throws at you, because it comes from inside.

Then nothing matters very much. Then you can die. Everything is all right. You could die or they could mug your neighbour, it is okay. You will help the neighbour but you will not get too upset about it because everything is interesting. Al Hamdulillah, everything is interesting.

We have lost our curiosity. Our curiosity is the only freedom we have. It does not matter what happens. Its blessing and its curse are in equal measures and ultimately it is all blessing. You know nothing of this path if you have not understood that.

Shaykh Ali al-Jamal said that the meaning of the thing is hidden in its opposite. Look at the worst times of your life and the biggest disasters, think back and say; 'Wasn't this the greatest blessing?' Didn't this make the most amazing difference? I would not have been able to know these things of life if that had not happened'. Think about the times when everything went well, when you had no complaints. How much did you learn about yourself and your own limitations at these times? The truth is that when things are going fine we learn nothing that really matters. The times when things are going well are the worst of times. When societies are wealthy they go flabby and they die **4**, and when societies are poor they develop strength. Soft times are bad for us and hard times are good for us. This is true for groups and individuals.

The meaning of a thing is hidden in its opposite. Now if you are clever about this it means that you do not have a vested interest in it whether it is a soft time or a hard time. You know that if a meaning of a thing is hidden in its opposite, then the opposite's meaning is the thing that you are in, and it is all interesting. It is all worthy of your curiosity. It is all a cycle.

When you have succeeded the success is dangerous to you because it makes you presumptuous and lazy, it becomes your failure. Your failure knocks you flat and you say 'I have got to get up and make it.' So you see, the one state is immediately the next state. That is why it does not matter to the faqir whether he is in the shade or in the sun. He knows that there is no such thing as permanent blessing and permanent curse. The whole of existence oscillates. It does not matter. The issue is not to be depressed because it is now dark and you are unhappy, because it will be light tomorrow. The true skill is to be curious about it. Let it in, stop judging it.

In the Qur'an Allah speaks of warfare saying that it has been ordained for you and it may be that you do not like something which is good for you. So use this month of Ramadan as a month of shutting-down, of disconnecting yourself, of breaking the habits. It is one of the key blessings of Ramadan, that cup of coffee; you cannot have it now. That glass of coke that you would have at 10 O'clock in the morning or at 3 O'clock in the afternoon, you cannot have it now. You have to become passive. Not the judge but the judged, not the one who is forging the world but the one who is being moulded by the world. Not the one who changes the other but the one who is being changed like a clay sculpture in the hands of the One and Only Sculptor.

The more you stop being in charge the more He becomes in charge. The more you silence yourself the more He illuminates you and then what comes out of you is Light. What comes out of you is not from you, it is from Allah. If you continue with this path and on this journey you will start seeing patches of light. You will experience moments when clearly it is not you talking, when you know it is not you talking because it is too profound. You are as surprised at what is coming out of you as you would be if it came out of somebody else and this increases over time.

Shaykh Fadhlallah has written two tracts of short of aphorisms and poems. One is called 'Bursts of Silence' and the other one is called 'Bursts of Light'.

Understand that these two conditions are synonymous. The more silent you are the more light you have. To swim in this silent light is to be alive and to be free. Not to live in this light is to suffer the imprisonment of the walking dead.

May Allah grant us success on the path.
May Allah grant us nearness to Him.
May Allah grant us annihilation in Him.
May Allah grant us death before we die.

Al Hamdulillah.

2: F.A. - Our assumptions displace the person. When we stereotype we are engaging our assumption, not the other.
3: A.A. - "Increase me in bewilderment of Thee!"
4: F.A. - Good times can breed complacency and stagnation.

Consciousness: Moment by Moment
Discourse 3: 9 November 2001

Bismillahir Rahmanir Rahim:

We learn from the Rasul (s.a.w.s.) that he said, from Allah, that if there was the slightest measure of good which is ordained for you, then nothing can stop that from coming to you. If there is the slightest element of harm which He has intended for you, that you could do nothing to avoid that harm. We are completely His creatures, not just in the physical shapes that we have and our features, or our skin tones, or our height, or our size, or our agendas. These were not the only things that were decreed before endless time.

We are also his creatures in terms of who we decide to be as people in this life. Who we are as people in this life is how we act and how we respond to events. All of that is part of the decree. Before endless time He fashioned the being that is you, and every moment that you are alive He chips away at your being. He chips away at your being like a sculptor making a sculpture. He uses the chisel of the moment to score you and to mark you in such a way that your character comes out, that your character appears.

The only choice that we have in the matter is either to accept what He is doing to us or to resist it. We accept by approaching every moment with taqwa. Taqwa means fear of Allah. This implies both a sense of conviction of His overawing and continuous presence and carefulness, a knowing that He is in charge and what has been presented to you has come from Him; it has come from nowhere else. A knowing that in the moment that He has given to you there is a secret and if you respond correctly, with ihsaan and with sincerity, the next piece of the puzzle of your existence and of your being will come to the fore and unfold.

This means that you trust Him. It means that you trust that what He gives to you in your life is for your own good. The other way of responding to the moment that He has put in front of you is to try to prevent it or resist it. There are a hundred ways in which one can prevent being in the moment and dealing correctly with what Allah gives you in that moment.

The most common way we do this is to want something else, and one of the ways in which we want something else is by having an idea in our mind about what we think we want. When Allah puts in front of us something which is unpleasant or something which we are trying to avoid we attempt to evade it because we think we know better. For example, you are required to deal with a family member who has done something unjust, but because you do not want to upset the harmony of the family or wish to appear disloyal, you do not speak about it. You think that you can manage the affair in such a way that this whole mess which you had to speak out against would be covered up. That is not rising to the challenge that He has given you in the moment.

When you rise to whatever He has given you in the moment, you allow Him to chisel you. You accept the blows that He is giving you because you realise that the blow is about you becoming yourself. You do not complain about the hardness of the blow because you recognise that it is for you. It enables you to become, to appear, like a sculpture coming out of stone. Sir Henry Moore once said that when he sculpts a horse he takes away all the rock that does not look like a horse. This is what Allah does with us. He calls us out of undifferentiated existence by impacting on us with events. The events are His hammer and His chisel. With these He gives us our shape and our form.

So in you there is this divinely sculptured original being and what allows the being to come out of the mass of nothingness in the rock is Allah's chipping another piece of the rock away in every moment. He chips another piece of what you are not away so that the essence of who you are can emerge. The essence of what you are can not come out if you do not allow the chisel and the hammer to fall; in other words, if you try and change the blow or if you resist what is happening. It is when we resist that life becomes dangerous to us and actually does fundamental damage.

Allah says that all good comes from Him and all harm comes from ourselves. You harm yourself when you do not accept what He is putting you through. You want to change your destiny; you want to dodge the blows. By dodging the blows you put yourself at cross-purposes to the blows and that is when you get broken. It is as if the rock that the sculptor is trying to sculpt has a mind of its own. As the hammer comes down to sculpt the rock at the right place, the rock moves trying to avoid the blow and the thing that was going to be a nose gets knocked off. So by interfering you can only settle for less than the best. By not accepting what He is doing to you, you are settling for less than the best. He truly is in charge. Truly. Al Hamdulillah!

We are His creatures. So, the art of being alive is the art of living unconditionally. Living unconditionally means you do not present life with a list of expectations, but you accept what has been ordained for you. You are unconditional in your gratitude for what has been given. This unconditional gratitude enables unconditional behaviour, and the more unconditional you are in terms of how you behave the freer you become. The more conditional you are the more miserable you become.

If I have my fixed ideas about what will make me happy, my happiness is dependent on that condition. For example, I convince myself that I will not be happy unless I have silver plating on my car. Which means while the silver plating is not there I am unhappy. And even if I should get the silver plating, because all conditional states are in a state of decay, I now spend my life being distressed about the tarnishing of the silver. So other than the brief moment when I have just received the silver plating, my expectation for silver plating has caused me nothing but misery.

We may say, 'but who would be so silly as to want a silver plated car', but this is beside the point. What condition we have circumscribed for our fulfillment is irrelevant. The root of the ill is that our motive is conditional.

So going back to the car, firstly while I do not have silver plating on my car I am miserable and secondly everything that I do is aimed at getting silver plating on my car. Every action that I undertake is laced through the intention; laced with the condition of wanting to get that silver plating, not realizing that Allah has decreed for me a car with gold plating and diamonds. His decree is better than I could ever have wished for, but I blocked that possibility because I was settling for my own ideas, my own expectations and assumptions. We cannot do better for ourselves than He can do for us. We are not able to be more ingenious than He is.

In a sense Allah asks us to look back at our lives and to ask 'am I truly a self-made person?' If you answer yes to this question you are not only a kafir and an ingrate, you are an idiot because you do not then recognize how deeply indebted you are to things that came from other than you. Clearly all of us had things happening to us in our lives which made the best in us possible, things which were completely outside of our control and which we tried to avoid happening to us at the time. You could not have designed who you have become. Your form shows marks of genius which is bigger than your own ingenuity.

When you were 5 years old you could not have looked forward into your life and made a plan that said: 'Well, when I am 18 years old I would have done this and that, and when I am 20 years old I would have done this and that, and when I am 30 I would have done that and by 45 this, and by 75 I would have achieved all of the following.' It is not possible. This means that your life has a design to it that is bigger than your own ability to plan. It is not up to you to work the whole thing out. In fact very often the major life changing events, the events that had the most profound impact on where your life went, were in a sense chosen for you. The only thing you had power over was how you responded to them.

So when you look back at your life, recognize that you have not been in charge. Recognize that you have been the recipient of blessings too infinite to measure, the sum of which has produced you as you are today. This means that you also recognize that whenever you have tried to take charge you messed everything up. Why is this so?

Taking charge means you have the conviction that if you do not take control, the outcome of what is in process will not be good enough. There are two discourtesies in this. Firstly, you are saying that what is there is not good enough, which is really an expression of ingratitude. Secondly you are saying I do not trust where this is going into the future which is why I need to interfere. Our relationship with each other is a metaphor for Allah's relationship with us. Assume that you are dealing with a rather stubborn person who you were trying to help, and everything you did for that person was greeted with discontentment and suspicion. How long would you continue being nice to that person? How can one expect flagrant ingratitude and distrust to be greeted with generosity?

Gratitude to and trust in Allah are therefore the two key qualities which form the basis of a successful life. They both have to do with your demeanour as you look at the two directions of time, namely past and future, forward and backward.

When you are looking into your past the only correct demeanour should be gratitude. If you are looking into your past and do not feel gratitude, understand that you are not seeing the thing as it is. Worse, when you look into your past with ingratitude you only see blemishes. 'Oh well, that one did this nasty thing to me when I was so old where that one did this horrible thing to me, and you know it has scarred me for life. But it really is typical. I always have been the victim of injustices that I had no control over.'

But what about all the things that worked? When I look at the past with ingratitude my eye glosses over these things. They are not nearly as interesting as the awful things. But you know, insofar as I am still alive more things must have worked than did not work. There had to be more function than dysfunction. Had this not been the case I would be dead. If there is more dysfunction than function to my liver then it no longer works. It is a dead liver. This must therefore be true for my body and by extension my whole life. Insofar as I am alive it is evidence that life works. Al Hamdulillah!

No matter how terrible the thing was that happened to you, you are still alive now. It did not kill you. So there is more good than bad. More function than dysfunction. We have said this before a hundred times, you cannot account for the metabolism of you spleen. You cannot make your liver work. All of these things work without you taking charge of them. You would not be here today if it were not for your lungs. You do not make yourself work. We either get out of the way and allow our life to work, or interfere and make ourselves sick.

For you to have arrived at this point where you are now there has to have been, by definition, infinitely more blessings than curses, otherwise you would not be alive. Not to recognize this i naive.

A human being that looks back at his life with a sense of rancour and disappointment and anger is deluded. He is not seeing things as they are. When you look back upon your life from the viewpoint of it all being bad and that all the things that happened to you were wrong, and from the point of view of having been made a victim, you become dangerous.

You will spend all of your time in the future to redress the perceived iniquities of your past, to get your own back. You cannot act correctly if you feel that the world has done you in; your natural reaction is going to be to want to do the world in. The last person whom you can trust is somebody who has a score to settle. When a person's behaviour is based on gratitude they don't have a score to settle so they can be trusted. When a person feels that life has done them in they have a score to settle. You can't trust a person who has a score to settle.

We are all very affected by the psychology of the age. The psychology of the age is the psychology of the victim. We seem to have agreed that the victim is somehow noble. 'Oh, he was so oppressed, how terrible. What a shame, the poor man.'

Understand that the victim is a monster. A victim feels that because he has been done in the world owes him and he is going to get his own back. You cannot trust a victim. No matter how legitimate the victim's accusation is, while he carries that accusation he is a very dangerous person. While a person feels done in he feels it is legitimate to get his own back. **5.** In a sense he blames his own unjust action on the other. He is saying 'I am doing this to you because of what they have done to me. You see, it really is all your fault. I am not accountable'.

It is the same with all of us. Say we have a fish business and one of the partners in the business wanted to get some money from the Department of Trade and Industry which was free, insofar as anything like this is ever really free. He wanted a loan to start the business. No strings attached, you do not have to pay back, and why? Because most of the people involved in this business are designated as previously disadvantaged individuals. As soon as something like this happens, don't touch it with a bargepole.

You then take on yourself the status of the disadvantaged.**6.** You take on the psychology of the disadvantaged. The psychology of the disadvantaged is ignoble. Who says that you are or have ever been disadvantaged? How can you be disadvantaged? Does your spleen work? Does your liver work? Have the very difficulties from your past not enabled qualities such as patience, perseverance and struggle? How can you view yourself as disadvantaged? Allahu Akbar! What a charge against life. What an accusation against Allah.

We have all heard about the story that there are two ways of looking at a glass with water in it. You can either say that the glass is half full or that the glass is half-empty. Now, if we look back upon our lives, we are dealing with a barrel full of water and one barrel has got maybe one, two or three drops of water less than another barrel. The water in the barrel is the barakat, the blessing of your life and the one, two or three drops which are missing are the few incidents of oppression that you have suffered. What about the rest of the barrel?

Everybody has got their miserable story to tell, the rich and the poor. If you listen to the story of a rich person he will tell you that he has a life of privilege, and this has been his curse. I have heard people say that. He will say that he was not allowed to mix or play with other kids, and that it all was so awful, that it caused so much misery in his life. You will speak to another person and he will say that he grew up in the ghetto and how it has ruined his life. So it does not matter who you are. We all have our miserable story to tell. Your privilege is your curse and your being underprivileged is also your curse. Stop viewing it as a curse. Say: *"Al Hamdulillah!"*

If I lived with privilege it may enable me to learn that the really important things in life, such as love, patience, gratitude, restraint, nobility and honour have no price. If I came from the underprivileged I would have learned some humanity, and humility. Everything has a blessing. See the blessing, and not the curse. Do not ever behave as if you are owed. You are owed nothing. You are not even owed the breath you are about to take in. It is all by Allah subhanahu wa ta'ala's decree, it is all bil'llah.

Now when you have the status of one that is not owed you can look into the future with no expectations. It is only when you feel owed that you have expectations. If you go to your neighbour and your neighbour owes you some money, you go there with the expectation that he is going to give you some money. If you say he owes you nothing then there is no expectation, then if he gives you money, Al Hamdulillah! What a gift!

What pleasure is there in getting something you are owed? If you drink tea and cannot appreciate the tea you have not really enjoyed it.

In fact you have not really experienced it. Anything that you experience which is not experienced with appreciativeness and gratitude is not really experienced at all. To eat what you feel is owed to you is to eat dust. To eat what you are grateful for is to eat honey. This status of being the victim robs people of the sweetness of life.

What makes it possible to look at the future with no expectations is that you trust what Allah is bringing to you. You trust that He has better in store for you than what you could have for yourself. Why do you have that trust? You have looked back at your life with wisdom and you have seen the extraordinary things that have happened. You recognize that your life is extraordinary, that it is miraculous and that it is magnificent. These qualities are not just true for the big things, like having become Muslim; it is true for the very small things as well. Like the fact that your tear ducts work and keep your eyes moist. Amazing! This life of yours is magnificent and it is bigger than you. The only appropriate thing to say about your life, no matter how apparently underprivileged is *"Al Hamdulillah!"*, *"Subhaanallah!"* I could not have done this, so therefore I trust that what He is going to give me is correct, and it is the best for me, and it is infinitely better for me than what I can plan for myself. At this time it is very easy for us to become morbid because there are all these things going on, the Americans and the awful things happening in Afghanistan, even the state of the crime in our own country. If you want to be depressed you don't have to look very far to find an excuse.

A key skill on this path is to mind your own business, because if you mind your own business and leave the rest to Allah you will see that there is only blessing. If you do not experience blessing moment by moment in your life, understand that you are not minding your own business. You are putting your nose into things that you should not. If you are dealing with things that have got nothing to do with you, you will get depressed and you will get miserable. A measure of whether you are dealing with things which have got nothing to do with you is the degree to which you are depressed and miserable.

Understand that Allah writes moment by moment, like the script of the most incredible play, like a massive piece of theatre, and it is written for you, an audience of one. If you look at it from that point of view ask yourself 'what is He telling me? What blessing is there in this? How must I interpret this?', then you really start reading and you will see wonder upon wonder.

Shaykh Muhammad Ibn al Habib said that all created things are meanings set up as images. As the thing is presented to you, you only perceive its form. Its true reality is the meaning behind the form. Learn to read that text and you will be too enchanted to be depressed. Rely on the Great Sculptor. Rely on Allah to turn you into the magical being that He has designed you to be.

———
May Allah grant us success on the path.
May Allah grant us nearness to Him.
May Allah grant us annihilation in Him.
May Allah grant us death before we die.

Al Hamdulillah.

———

5: F.A. - This also creates the condition for people to become opportunistic.

6: T.S. - The business subsequently failed because of the self gratifying behaviour of this person.He did himself in, in the end!

FREEING THE BREATH
Discourse 4: Undated

Bismillahir Rahmanir Rahim:

Things really aren't as they seem. We're confronted by a world of objects that creates the illusion of solidity. Things you can grasp and manipulate and wield and apply and manage to your own benefit and to your own ends. The reality of the matter is far more subtle than that. That which your eyes see and which your hands feel is an assumption of solidity. It is in fact something very tenuous; the reason for this is that the vehicle of perception, which is the body and the self, via your eyes, your hands and your ears, are all very tenuous.

One of the significances that one can tease out of the hadra is an examination of breath. Your whole capacity to act and think and interact with the world is based on something as ethereal as a lung full of air. Seal off that lung full of air and the whole theatre of that capacity collapses like a house of cards. Therefore the apparent solidity and capacity is underpinned by something very subtle which you cannot see, which is light, which has no weight, which is your breath. Your solidity is underpinned by, and gets its substance from, that which is imperceptible. This is not 'sufispeak', this is not referring to the realm of the unseen, this is as it is. If I held my hand over your mouth long enough, you would not be able to pick up the stick and shout at the child and reach for the water. You would be dead.

This means that what underpins the complexity of the world around you is something very fine and subtle. That very fine and very subtle thing is something which you cannot take charge of. In fact one of the major causes of disease is when people interfere with their breath. Most of us do not breathe properly. We interfere with our breath, principally on the basis of fear. When we are frightened we don't breathe naturally, we hold our breath in the same way that we want to hold onto our life. So we choke ourselves.

This means to say that interfering with breath, which is interfering with the very subtle essence of life, is the first act of illusion. It is the companion to the claim to be able to manage your own affairs. There's nothing more natural than breathing. Animals are quite natural with their breath, while human beings aren't. Human beings don't breathe correctly. This is because most humans have learnt the habit, based on fear, of interfering with their breath; of wanting to take charge of the affair. Is it not interesting that the very quality that makes us human, the capacity to speak, is concerned with interrupting breath?

Speaking is about defining things, which is about delineating and circumscribing things; making them solid; giving them form. It is fear that wants to make everything solid, make everything concrete and make everything graspable. When you can grasp a thing you can control it; the more subtle a thing is, the less you can grasp it. You can grasp the stick because it has hard edges. You can't grasp water; it does not have the same shape and form.

The nature of the subtle is that it cannot be grasped, it cannot be held, and it cannot be made safe and non-threatening. This means that our assumption of being in charge of our lives, of reducing it to manageable things that you can grasp, is based on an illusion.7 Managing is based on manipulating; manipulating is based on that which you can lay your hands on. It implies taking things and reducing them to solidity, freeze them so that you can hold them, grasp them.

Unfortunately life is not based on solidity, it is based on fluidity. Even rocks flow with the passage of time, continents move with the passage of time, stars come into being, and solar systems collapse or explode. There is nothing solid with the passage of time. By time everything is going to be changed, is going to be vanquished, is going to lose its 'graspability', it is going to lose its solidity. While we assume we can take control over the affair and assume we can reduce things to a manageable state that we are in charge of, we are contradicting the very essence of our own lives, because we can't take charge of our breath and when we do we get sick. When you act contrary to the design you get sick, and grasping contradicts the essence of the world around us.

And so we become beings that are at cross purposes to existence, we are against the flow. We become battered. We don't age with grace; we don't develop a sense of fulfilment and peace in our lives. The very structure of our selves contradicts the passage of life itself. If only we knew that what Allah has in store for us is better than what we can have in store for ourselves. If only we knew that if we gave up what we are trying to hold on to, the surprise which would come to us from that is much bigger and much better than the thing we wanted. The direction which existence is flowing into will be far better than the thing you are trying to manage.

The significance of saying 'don't manage the affair' is to leave the managing of the affair to Allah. That doesn't imply you should behave like an idiot, or become catatonic and sit in your corner. It means do what you can to the best of your ability on the basis of what you consider to be the right thing to do and the rest is not up to you. Know by definition that you are in the middle of a series of events, of an incalculable orchestration of events, which are not in your capacity to take charge of.**8**

You can't take charge of your body. You can't tell your liver to stop working. You can take things to make it stop working, but you can't command it. You can't command your bone marrow to produce red blood cells. You can't command the alveoli in your lungs to absorb oxygen or to expel carbon dioxide. You are in the middle of a series of events, all of which sustain your existence, which you can't take charge of. Now if you can't take charge of a single alveolus in your lungs to take in oxygen, how on earth do you think you are going to take charge of your life? It's not possible. We can't take charge of our lives. We can't manage the affair, it's far too complex, and it's far too subtle and far too fluid.

The very attempt to manage it, to grasp it, to lay a hand on it to bend it to your will, is to do it violence. It has the same effect as interfering with your breath. So the managing of the affair in the outer is the same thing as not breathing naturally. Your inner disease is based on fear, and is an inner interference with your breath. It has an outer equivalent manifestation and that is a interference with the flow of life, wanting to take charge of life. The fear which interferes with the breath, is the same fear which underlies your wanting to contain the other so that the other does not become threatening. Controlling the other, laying a hand on the other, chaining the other all stems from fear which means not trusting in Allah.

This means to say that letting go of the other, freeing the other, confronting your fear and learning how to be naturally yourself, learning how to breathe and learning how to be comfortable in your body is the same thing. Allah tells us in Surah Al Asr **9**: *"By time man is at a loss, except those who believe"*. Now what is belief? It's an inner state. Belief means that 'I know that there is a manager in charge'. In Nguni languages the words for belief and trust are the same. Ukuthemba. To believe is to trust. I trust that I no longer have to manage the affair because it is being managed by ingenuity infinitely greater than mine.

Belief is an inner peace. I can't do myself any good if He does not want to do it to me. I can't do myself any harm if He does not want to do it to me. It's in His hands; it's out of my hands. So I can relax and I can breathe easy. This is imaan. Imaan is inner wholesomeness, an inner wholesomeness which is based not on a fear of existence but a trust of existence.

But Allah says that's not good enough, you not only have to have inner correctness, you also need to have amalus-salihaat, outer correctness. And outer correctness means dealing with the world with kindness and not with brutality.

It means feeding the orphan, moving the stone, lifting the baggage and smiling at the person. So that the hand that grasps the world is a gentle hand, a non-interfering hand. This is not to say you are an idiot and a push-over. When someone requires correcting, you correct them.

However, you are not correcting them on the basis that 'I have to fix the world', because you are not here to fix the world, He is there to fix the world. It is His Existence. You are the audience in the theatre. You are not the writer of the script. You are not busy managing the outcome of a more equitable world tomorrow. You are paying your dues in the moment you are in. You are doing what He requires from you right now because you know that is the toll that you need to pay to continue on the path he has laid out for you. Correct action in the moment you are in is the toll we have to pay to stay on this exhilarating, transforming and ravishing ride that he has laid out for us.**10**

To sum this up: There are incalculable implications to the twin charges of belief and correct action, and at a subtle level both of these things deal with fear and the acting out of this fear. The fear eventually starts to interfere with your inner working, interferes with your breathing and ultimately with your inner wholesomeness.**11** Not only do you choke yourself but you grab the world by its throat in order to control it. Both of these attempts are diseased. If your own choking of yourself doesn't take you out with a heart attack, then someone else who you are trying to choke will come and take you out by putting a hole through your head. And it's because you earned that retribution, through fundamentally denying your responsibility which is to be on this roller coaster of this existence in order to enjoy the ride.

You have been made to worship. Worshipping means that you are amazed and in awe. You can't be in awe if you are trying to keep the thing under wraps all the time. You can only be in awe if you are part of the rush, part of this whole play that is on this incredible journey of transformation and change.

———

May Allah grant us freedom from our own fear.
May Allah make us aware of Him as our constant Companion.
May He make us companionable with Him.
May Allah grant us conversation with Him and comfort in Him
May Allah grant us a gentle hand with the world around us.
May Allah grant us a just hand with the world around us.
May Allah grant us nearness to him.
May Allah grant us annihilation.
May Allah grant us death before we die.

Al Hamdulillah.

———

7: F.A. - All reductionism is about makingthat which is subtle manageable.

8: F.A. - This impliesthat submission is effort. It is a conscious choice,not the act of a victim.

9: The Qur'an, chapter 103.

10: A.A. - Knowing that the particular moment you are in contains the secret to the next stage ofunfoldment – that is trust.

11: F.A. - Diseased; Opposing peace.

Not Knowing
Discourse 5: Undated

Bismillahir Rahmanir Rahim:

In conversation if you catch yourself saying the same thing three or four times, then know what is at issue is no longer that which you are trying to say, but the attention you are trying to capture from the other. There are two ways in which our attention can function, one way either finds the other interesting and the other attempts to get the other to find the self interesting.

The attempt to get the other to affirm the self always results in failure. Any attempt by the self to claim significance immediately calls conflict from the other because it's a fundamental perversity. We have not been made to find ourselves significant. We have been made to find Allah and His extraordinary creation significant. Our attention has been sculpted in such a way that it is built to face outwards. Your eyes are not made to look into the back of you skull, that would look ugly, wouldn't it? Your eyes are made to be pointed to the other. You see there's a fundamental sense of perversity in trying to claim significance of any kind. It is an ugliness to which the other is programmed to be hostile.

There is nothing more depressing than a company of people who are all clamouring to be heard. It is as if none of them realize the secret of Shaykh Ali al Jamal which is that silence has pre-eminence over speech. In other words the one who listens has power over the one who speaks. In fact the party who defines the nature of the transaction is never the one doing the speaking, but always the one doing the listening.

And it does not matter what the truthfulness of the speaker is, how accurate, philosophically sound or theologically sound the one who is speaking is, he is at the mercy of the listener. All the listener has to do is shift their attention slightly and the one who is speaking is deflated and reduced to futility. So the one who is observing is far more significant than the one who is attempting to be observed. And not only is the one who is observing more significant, he also becomes the ascendant.

There is a wonderful story that Shaykh Abdal Qadir used to tell repeatedly about Imam Khomeini and the Shah of Iran. Just prior to the Shah's demise he was crowned Shahan-Shah, which means king of kings. He ascended this huge throne and had a gilded crown placed on his head that was so heavy it almost broke his little neck. The ceremony was conducted with the most awe inspiring pomp and circumstance. Shaykh Abdal Qadir read about this event in a newspaper.

A week after this article appeared the same newspaper carried another article of Imam Khomeini. The article included a photograph of Imam Khomeini in sajdah. Shaykh Abdal Qadir said that that was when he knew the matter was over. Within a couple of weeks the Shah was deposed and the Imam was in charge. The one who disclaims significance is made significant. The one who claims significance is destroyed.

You'll find this principle repeated over and over. One of the most powerful popes of the Roman Catholic Church was a man called Benedict the Third; he lived in about the 12th century. This man had himself crowned as Caesar because he arrogated to himself leadership over the whole of Christendom. On a given Christmas day Benedict had himself ensconced on Constantine's throne, he had a laurel wreath placed on his head like the Roman emperors, got himself a sword and had himself proclaimed lord of the Roman Empire.

That claim was the beginning of the end of Catholic ascendancy in Europe. From that point forward Catholicism was in a decline, never again to regain the hold on Europe that it had before. As for Benedict, he died soon after. His body was exhumed by his successor and put on trial for the murder of his predecessor.

Vilification upon vilification; abuse upon abuse. Look at all of these great men; as soon as their greatness went to their heads, they were taken away. It may have taken a decade or two, but they were taken away.

At every turn, no matter who you are looking at, the Christians, the Jews or the Muslims, as soon as a person claims significance for himself he is destroyed.

All of this serves to demonstrate that we are here to worship. This means that we should not find ourselves significant, because that is a misuse of the self; it is doing violence to the self. It's like the mirror trying to look at itself. If it looked at itself it would snap or it would bend double. You are supposed to be the mirror of existence. You cannot be the mirror of existence if you keep finding yourself so incredibly significant, important and worthy of note.

This propensity we have to forget ourselves and who we really are is the core facet of the dysfunction of the human condition. We forget our truly graced status in the middle of the exist ence that we are in. We forget that we are charged with nothing other than to be in awe of it and to worship. This forgetfulness gets visited on us in a hundred little ways. The most dangerous way that it gets visited on us is any assumption that we have that we have worked it out: 'I now know it all; I have now worked it all out'. The moment you get onto your high horse of presumption, of self congratulation, you must know that the wake up call is speedily on its way. The further you are on this path, the quicker the wake up call is going to come, because when Allah loves you, He doesn't let you get away with mucking about. He very quickly visits upon you the idiocy of your situation, so that you can pull yourself straight.

That is why we very often see people who are clearly on the path being knocked about by life, and we may think to ourselves that this is not fair. 'He is such a good fellow, you know. He really should not have to suffer like this.' We are wrong. It is enormously fair, because Allah is not allowing that person any leeway for their mediocrity. As soon as they think they've got it worked out, or as soon as they quietly suspect that they really are very significant people, they get tripped up by an event that reminds them, and us of who we all really are: needy, bereft and unentitled supplicants.

The catastrophe is Allah saying 'come here let Me help you' and sooner or later this happens to all of us – we all face periods of being brought back down to earth and it is a mark of ill favour when He does not bring you down to earth quickly. So we should take counsel from Shaykh ad-Darqawi, that our difficulties are our best times, these times are when we are being brought back down to our status.**12**

Our peculiar condition is that when we've worked it all out, what we have worked out is that we understand nothing at all. The nature of the matter is that it always escapes the realm of understanding. How can you be amazed if you are not surprised and can you be surprised if you know it all. If there isn't newness and freshness in what gets presented to you? In other words, without an element of surprise and amazement, an element of 'this is amazing, I didn't know that', our demeanour is dismissive. Then everything gets reduced to what you already know.**13**

When there's nothing more to know then we might as well die. So unless you can look with an innocent eye at the world around you and truly see that which you haven't yet understood in every minute that passes you by, then you are not seeing the thing as it is. You are not really alive. Not to see the thing as it is, not to be bewildered by it, is a misapplication of your life. You have been made to be enawed and to worship. This condition is inconsistent with being bored. Instead of approaching each situation with caution and an attempt to understand it, we rather take a cursory glance at it and dismiss it with an attitude of 'I already know this'. In this way we miss essential details which would challenge who we think we are. Most of us trivialise the world around us. We regard this thing in front of us as insignificant and ordinary, not realising that it is from Allah and is therefore by definition extraordinary. We dismiss what our Rabb has put in front of us with an off-hand, 'oh I know this' attitude. **14**

Every moment whatever Allah puts in front of me He puts in front of me for one reason, so that I can take the next step forward in my growth. The next step in my growth shows me where I am not. In other words every moment in front of me confirms my insufficiency, my lack of actually knowing it or of being self sufficient. The calibration of my eye should be to read the moment so that I can see what I haven't yet come to grips with.

Every moment has that nature. Every moment has within it a challenge, something which I've not yet cracked. Part of the reason why I don't see what's in front of me, is because I have my own assumption of what's standing in front of me. It's like the story of the Loreley, who were the mythical creatures on the Rhine who made wailing sounds and completely enchanted sailors. They use to find these sounds so alluring that they got drawn to their deaths.

We're like the sailors on the Rhine that hear the Loreley. We have something on our minds but clearly there is something else going on. Our lives are like that: we have one thing on our minds, but there is something else going on. However, Allah is a bit more forgiving than what the Loreley were. When the child walks into the throne and then abuses the king the only reason the child is still alive afterwards is that the king has an incredibly merciful nature.

We only exist by the mercy of Allah, because if you consider that He is All-Encompassing, it means that He is present, He is before us, behind us, within us, beside us, in front of us. He completely encapsulates us. It is as if we live in a matrix of Allah. We do not have an independent existence from Him, the breath that comes into us He blows into us, the breath that comes out of us He sucks out of us. He commands the chemical reactions that make the energy available for us to move our limbs. He is the essence of your essence, you cannot escape Him. **15**

Yet we think we live independently and we somehow have our own power. In other words your assumption of being an individual is false, because you are not an individual; you're this dizzy swirl of atomic material that has this vague shape called a human being. And this atomic material gets replaced very quickly. It is a very vague shape, very indistinct. This crispness that you assign to your own self is not there.

So why should we have this bizarre view that we exist independently. This can only be because Allah withholds His nature from us. If you were to truly know in your being that you are not separate from others you would also see that your independent existence was false.

Allah withholds His nature from us which enables the illusion that we exist independently of Him. He veils us from Him.

There's this crushing weight of the universe which should crush us. The only reason why this does not happen is because it's literally being held up, away from us. So the king does not have the child's head knocked off because the king is merciful, he is kind and generous. He wills the best for the child and is patient. He withholds the implications of his majesty from the child. But this is not because it is what the child deserves. The child deserves to have his head knocked off. And so do we.

We deserve nothing other than annihilation, complete and utter annihilation. We are only here by Grace; by permission.

We are here because He chose to share His nature with us. Our position in the centre of the affair is not an earned position. It is a grace and a blessing. I am a very small being surrounded by momentous things, any one of which could and should annihilate me yet does not. The implications of my smallness in the face of the awesome are withheld from me, for a while, so that I can see how awesome it is. I can be in awe. I can worship.

So the practice of being human is the practice of worship. And that means that you understand in every moment that stands before you that you don't know. You look at it with fresh eyes and you are surprised because you see His hand in it. That can only happen if you stop paying attention to your own inner dialogue, so that you can give due attention to the moment that faces you, in an innocent and unpresumptuous way.

It is to that end that we do acts of worship. It is to that end that we do dhikr. It is to that end that we do salah. All of these, if they serve their purpose, will deliver you to a quiet place. That place is a silencing of your inner dialogue. If there is no noise inside, there's nothing to be said. If there's nothing to be said you can't fall into the error of wanting to be significant. The most companionable people are people you can sit with, without having anything to say and it is fine and you can still enjoy the tea, the company, without the chatter.

———

May Allah grant us success on the path.
May He grant us nearest to Him.
May He grant us annihilation in Him.
Allah, grant peace and blessings on our Nabi (s.a.w.s.)

Al Hamdulillah.

———

12: A.A. - Inability to comprehend IS comprehension!

13: F.A.- This is the arrogance of the age.

14: F.A. - This is about readingthe text that surrounds you.

15: F.A. - The Quran: *"To Allah belongs the East and the West; Whithersoever you turn, there is the presence (face) of Allah, for Allah is the All Pervading, the All Knowing."* [2:115].

Patience and Gratitude: The Sign of Imaan
Discourse 6: Undated

Bismillahir Rahmanir Rahim:

There really are only two ways of being in the world: one of darkness and the other of light, although one often sees a mix of the two. It is as if Allah has made darkness and light and then He has made grey, which is a mixture between darkness and light. This means that in essence it is all about understanding the difference between darkness and light. This distinction one can refer to as the distinction between living in the darkness of kufr and living in the light of imaan.**16**

Kufr as you know means to cover the truth; it comes from the root word, which means to cover. So it means to hide something. Now what is that truth that kufr hides? The truth is that there has to be a Designer behind all of the things that you see, otherwise they couldn't work. Life works. Why is it that planets are kept in their orbit, that the moon is kept in its place, that the sea- sons come and go, that your body has a rhythm and that your circulatory system has a design to it? Your neural system has a design to it, your muscles have a design, and your skeleton has a design.

Where does all this design come from? It can't have been by an accident, there has to have been a designer. To say that it is all by accident, that there is no designer, is both stupid and illogical. It covers the obvious reality that as soon as something demonstrates design, it invokes an idea of the designer. Design by definition is only design if it is deliberate. There is no such thing as an accidental design. If I take you and submit you to an accident, you no longer have design, you have brokenness, there is a bone sticking out of your body, there is blood on the floor. That's accident. Accident is the opposite to design. So kufr means to say that life has no design. It is all accidents, it is all about facts and matter, and things that you can measure and control.

Imaan says Allah exists. That there is far more to existence than the eye can see; the universe has a sense of design to it which is bigger than our own ability to explain. This is why the kafir and the Muslim are fundamentally different, because the kafir has and lives in a different world. He has covered the first assumption. The first premise that makes the believer's life tolerable is that he accepts as a given that whatever happens to him is right, it should have happened because there is a design to existence. The kafir says it is all accident.

Because the kafir says it's all accident, he has to make sure that accidents don't happen to him, so he spends his life taking out insurance, and taking out insurance isn't about just signing a contract with an insurance company. Taking out insurance is all the things that you do to guarantee your good fortune. Everything you do to get an outcome is fundamentally about insurance; it is something that you want to achieve in the future. As soon as you try to claim ownership over an outcome you are denying His Lordship because He is the Lord of outcomes.

You have no power over outcomes. You can pursue anything that you like, if it is not in your taqdir you will not get it. Allah tells us, if there is the smallest item of harm that is aimed at you, there is nothing in the world that you can do that will avoid that happening to you. If there is the smallest amount of good that will happen to you there is nothing in the world that will stop it happening to you. We have no power over outcomes.

So why does the kafir need to have power over the outcome? Well, his view is: 'if I don't look after myself no one else will. So I have to look after me, because the universe is out to get me. The world is a dangerous place; it's full of accidents'.

The Believer knows that he doesn't have to worry about the outcomes because there is a Lord of outcomes. It's not his job to worry about outcomes. His life has a design to it and that design he can trust. So he doesn't busy himself with things that are in fact a waste of his time. He doesn't busy himself trying to influence things that he has no influence over. He busies himself with those things that he can influence and he can influence what his Lord commands him to do in the moment. 'What is it that my Lord wants me to do? What is it that He wants me to put in, to give away? How can I serve Him?'

Because the kafir doesn't trust life, the kafir approaches life from a point of view of how life can serve him. 'What can I get from the world?' Because the mu'min trusts life, he approaches life from the point of view of how he can help. He says to himself: 'how can I serve my Lord, knowing full well that I am not here to serve myself and I am definitely not here for the world to serve me.'

We must understand that just having a Muslim name, and having professed the kalimah at some point, is not a guarantee against kufr. Kufr is not just an intellectual idea; it's a state in the heart. It is a state of worrying about outcomes, worrying about your self and not leaving outcomes to the Lord. One of the very first things I was taught being associated with a shaykh was that, if you have a problem, then leave it with Allah and He will take care of it. But if you try and fix that problem yourself, he will leave you to it. So everything you try and fix yourself is like an element of kufr.

Everything that you do which is about trying to look after your own interests is like being a kafir. You are belying your deen; you are belying your sajdah. Your sajdah says 'I am helpless'. Sajdah is an expression of being a Muslim, of being the submitted one, of witnessing that 'I have No Power'. You, Oh Allah, are the One with the Power. But then you come up from the musallah and you try to control people and try to make out of life what you want, therefore saying to the Lord that what You give me isn't good enough. I must get this or that, for myself.

We live in a time where being a kafir is viewed as being intelligent, quite literally. There are people who believe that it is primitive and medieval to try and find a designer behind the obvious design that you see in the world around you. They say it is all a result of accidents.

This is Charles Darwin's theory at work, and it gives them an excuse not to face the problem that there is a sense of design and the design is obviously beautiful and obviously praiseworthy.

Who is the one that should be praised? But if you say that this sense of design in fact is not a sense of design, it's just a lot of accidents that happen because of natural selection, and then you don't have to praise anyone.

What you must understand is that not to praise is like sewing up your mouth. To live and not to be grateful is like living a shadow, because surely to live means to experience. Think about eating a meal or drinking a cup of tea. When have you really experienced that cup of tea? When you have tasted it to the point of really appreciating it, or when you have just swallowed it down like it was just flavoured water? If you don't appreciate, the thing has lost its flavour, it has no taste.**17**

So the kafir lives in a world whose colours have become a black and white photograph. The smell has disappeared, the flavour of food has gone because he cannot find the one to whom he can say *"Al Hamdulillah"*-, to whom he can express his gratitude, to whom he can express his appreciation. You cannot show appreciation to accident; how do you say 'thank you'? How can an entirely random set of accidents account for the wonderful world we are in and how do we thank that which is blind, accidental and unconscious for this extraordinary gift called life?

So what we have to understand is that the kafir lives in a state of hell. You heard the story of Rasul (s.a.w.s.), when he was standing on the mimbar in Medina and he went into a state. His companions said *"Ya Rasulullah, what is the matter?"* and he replied *"I can sense Jannat, it is right here"*. Then he walked a few paces, then he went into a state and his companions asked *"What is the matter ya Rasulullah?"* He said *"I can feel the fires of Jehannam"*.**18** This implies that paradise and hell are not just on the other side of the grave.

They are proximate matters; these are things that we live with here. If you don't know how to be grateful, if you don't know how to recognize the sense of beauty and proportion and design and therefore give thanks to the Designer, your life is on fire, you are in a living hell. You are burning in your own discontentment, because the opposite of gratitude is discontentment, it is unhappiness. If you think your happiness is based on getting things, then you are thinking like a kafir. 'I'll only be happy if I get this or that.' That is mad. You take the same unhappy man and give him what he wants, he stays unhappy. Happiness isn't a function of achieving a goal, or money or anything else; happiness is the function of your gratitude. **19**

So to claim to be a Muslim and not to walk around in a world with a sense of wonder like a child, not being able to say Al Hamdulillah, Al Hamdulillah, a smile and kindness bubbling over to everyone you see, is to lie. You are not a Muslim. So these two ways of being, the darkness of kufr and the light of imaan have a very obvious sign. Their sign is gratitude.

How is a man who acts with gratitude, different from the man who acts with neediness, which is the opposite of gratitude? A man who acts from neediness is a slave; he is under the thumb of the world because he wants things from life. The one who acts from gratitude is not something that is empty and wants to be filled; it is a full thing that just empties. *"Hadha min fadli Rabbi"* **20**, 'this is from the over flowing of my Lord'. Every moment your dhikr should be *"Hadha min fadli Rabbi"*: This is from the over flowing of my Lord. You can die now, there is nothing more to get. Your heart is full and there is only the pleasure at seeing Him unfold His design.

———

May Allah grant us success in this world and the next.

May Allah grant us nearness to Him.

May Allah grant us annihilation in Him.

May He grant us death before we die.

Al Hamdulillah.

———

16: F.A. - The Qur'an: *"A.L.R. A scripture that we revealed to you, in order to lead the people out of the darkness into the light - in accordance with the will of their Lord - to the path of the Almighty, the Praiseworthy."* [14:1].

17: A.A. - This is a fundamental aspect of the sunna; to activate one's awareness, to be in the moment, to be fully 'here', to appreciate and to praise.

18: F.A. - Hell is a state that can be experienced now; it is not only symbolic of an end state.

19: F.A. - The Qur'an: *"Your Lord has decreed: The more you thank Me, the more I give you. But if you turn unappreciative, then My retribution is severe."* [14:7].

20: The Qur'an: [27:40].

ALLAH IS IN CHARGE
Discourse 7: 6 April 2001

Bismillahir Rahmanir Rahim:

Allah is in charge. Every human being will come to this realization at some point. The best of us and the worst of us, the most wicked and the most pious will all come to the same realization at some point. We will come to witness that there is a Manager to the entire affair. That He is the Being and the Presence in charge. However, some of us will arrive at that insight by choice and some of us will arrive at that insight by force. Arriving at that insight by choice is a description of Jannat. Arriving at that insight by force is a description of Jehannam.

A fire is a thing which consumes; which burns off impurities, which annihilates. If we have the assumption that we are in charge, then we are destined for the fire. Not because we are awfully wicked and the devil will come for us, but because that very way of looking at the world is the way of the fire. It is false. It is bound for destruction; it is bound for annihilation.

The worst nightmare to which you can subject a person who always wants to be in charge, is to tie their hands, their feet and their mouths up so that they cannot move, or do, or say anything. That is to incapacitate them to the point where they are completely without power. When they come to the coffin, they come to the point of complete powerlessness, they cannot resist anymore, and they cannot be in charge. That is the greatest horror of it all because they have attempted to be in charge their entire lives.

Here they get to a point where there is no argument. A corpse cannot argue back. A corpse cannot even tell his washer; listen, just move me this way or that way, I am very uncomfortable. Alternatively, could you please not expose my body like this? A corpse cannot do this. So we are all destined to a place of utter lack of volition. No choice. No capacity to object or resist.

For a person who thinks they can somehow be in charge of their lives that moment will be absolute, unmitigated horror. What we must understand about that horror is that it is timeless. This is so because the last moment is an empty moment. It does not have a back to it. Every moment that you are in has a moment behind it. When you die there is no moment after that. It empties; there is not a clock that ticks in the grave, tick, tock, it does not work like that.

There is no passage of time in the grave. It is timeless. It is beyond time. In other words, if you die in the state of rebellion against your powerlessness; that rebellion becomes infinite, that torture, that burning up is without end. It is Jehannam; endless burning, suffering.

It is very foolish to think that Jehannam is just a metaphor. Jehannam is literal, there is a place of eternal fire, and there is a place of eternal torment. In addition, that place is destined for those who did not believe. And who did not believe? Those who thought that they were in charge; those are the one's who did not believe.

If one understands it like this, you can also see that we all skirt very close to the edge of the pit. There are many hadith to this end. For example, the Rasul (s.a.w.s.) said; 'You can have a person who acts his entire life like a companion of the Garden and in their last moment, they behave like a person of the fire and they go to the fire. Then you can have a person, who acts their entire life like a companion of the fire, and in their last moment they behave like a person of the Garden, and they will be in the Garden.'

This means that you cannot trade with Allah because that is another way of trying to be in charge. Fixing the price; 'I will do so many virtuous things and earn so many thawab's. I will do this, I will do that, but in return You must give me Jannat. Subhaanallah. Who on earth do you think you are negotiating with? You cannot trade with Him. There is no trade. If you think that you can, you are irrevocably lost.

There is nothing to be gained. There is no contract to be called in. You cannot be in charge of the final outcome, because Allah is the Lord, not you.

We think those people who are kafir are the ones going to the fire. However, realise that assuming a capability to take charge is shirk.

Assuming you can take charge of an outcome is ascribing a partner to the Lord, because He alone is in charge of outcomes. If you make anything other than Allah significant, if you make anything other than Him the cause of things, you are in trouble. He is the only cause of things.

The disease of manipulating the world to achieve beneficial outcomes is very common. If you say to yourself that for you to have a good life you must get money, this is shirk. If you think that you will only be happy if you have a wife who is like this or like that, it is shirk. You can pray as much as you like, your intent remains shirk. If we think that we can do anything to attain the pleasure of Allah, like a contract for our own happiness, we are committing shirk. We are assuming we are in charge of our own good fortune. There is only One in charge.

Your own happiness, your total fulfilment is the pleasure of Allah. If you think that you can do it by yourself, then you are lost. It is not about doing it yourself. It is about submitting to allow Him to do it, because He is in charge. We are not here to be in charge, we are here to recognize that He is. That is all that He wants from us. We do that and He gives us the universe. The only reason He has made us is for us to know Him, in other words, to witness just how profoundly He is in charge. It is to say Subhaanallah, look, look, look at His traces, look at His signs, look at how He is in charge; beyond our ingenuity, look at how small our ingenuity is, and look at how small our creativity is next to His.

It is like that wonderful practice of the Persian carpet weavers, who deliberately weave a flaw into the carpet while every single stitch in the carpet has a dhikr pronounced on it. It is saying that in spite of this beauty it is in fact imperfect in the face of His Magnificence.

We are here to affirm that He is in charge of the entire affair. In addition, if He is in charge of the entire affair, He can do whatever He likes. He can take the biggest, worst, murdering, baby-liver eating sinner, and put him in the highest place in Jannat. He can take the most pious person and throw him into the deepest pits of Jehannam. That is the transcendent nature of the Presence that shadows us every moment that we are alive. If nothing else this should invoke a sense of carefulness and deliberateness, and not the offhand attitude of the haggling trader. What this Presence wants from us is to acknowledge His Magnificence, the fact that He is in charge, and that we cannot negotiate our future with Him. There is no price to be paid for what you have already received. How much less so can there be a price to be paid for what you are still going to receive? How can you ever return to Allah the blessings that you have already had in your life? Just for the function of your body, how are you going to repay Him? What rental are you going to pay for you liver, your hearing or your spleen? How are you going to repay Allah for the people in your life? How are you going to repay Him for having been able to witness the sunrise this morning; for being able to use your voice, for being able to drink a glass of water? You cannot pay for your existence. Clearly, if you cannot repay a thimbles worth of the ocean that you have already received, then the very idea that you can do the right things to earn a place in the hereafter is just outrageous.

This does not mean to say that we should not do the right things. We do the right things out of the spirit of worship; in gratitude. We do the right thing without keeping an account with Him. Keeping an account with Him is shirk. It is making some other thing absolute, other than Allah's Will. His Will is absolute; He is beyond law, He Creates the laws. He transcends the laws, and breaks them as He wills.

We are submitted to His decree. However, He is a generous Host because He has included as part of His decree the sustenance of every creature alive, unconditionally. Anything that exists comes from Him. So once you acknowledge that He is in charge, that acknowledgement is a safety; it is a protection. If He is the One who creates and sustains the sparrow, why will He not look after you?

Until recently the smallest of the denomination of South African coins had two sparrows on it. There is a story behind that. There was a family of Boer women who were locked up in the concentration camp at Bethulie during the Boer war. These women read a passage in the Gospel where Nabi Issa told a person that you could buy two sparrows for a farthing in the market, they were so worthless and yet your Lord looks after them. They leave their nest in the morning not knowing where they are going to be fed, and at night they return being fed. This story gave such comfort to these women that they made a pact that if they should survive the horror of the concentration camp they would campaign to have two sparrows put on the smallest denomination of the South African coin.

The next time that you handle a one cent coin, have a look at the two sparrows and know that if Allah can, in His Grandeur, be concerned with placing every single molecule correctly in that sparrow, so that everything works in it. Why would Allah Subahana wa'ta Allah not make your life work?

_____

May Allah grant us success on the path.
May He grant us nearest to Him.
May He grant us annihilation in Him.
Allah, grant peace and blessings on our Nabi (s.a.w.s.)

Al Hamdulillah.

GRATITUDE: CRACKING THE CODE
Discourse 8: 30 March 2001

Bismillahir Rahmanir Rahim:

We know that Allah made and created us because He loves to be known. This suggests that as long as our lives are concerned with witnessing Him, knowing Him, we will be in the centre of our purpose. Witnessing Him has an essence and an attribute. The essence is to see the perfection in what He has made, and the attribute is to act with an attitude of service from that station of being the one who is amazed at the perfection of what he witnesses.

Witnessing Him is to recognize His traces in the implicit sense of design in the world that surrounds you. If you can look at the leaf on a tree, at the wing of a fly, and say *"Subhaanallah"* then you are fulfilling the purpose of your being here. That is why He has made you. Everything else is a sideshow. Whatever you pursue as work, the earning of a living, raising of children or tending the sick, it is all incidental, it is not the essence. This is not, of course, to suggest that one should not do these things, like tending to the sick, feed the orphan or raise the children, but you do not tend to these things on the basis of having to fix it or of having to somehow make the world work.

If I am of the view that my project somehow makes things work, then I am dethroning Him and putting myself in His place. This is because I then claim to be the fixer. I am the one who is in charge when, in fact, it is the other way round. When I see His traces in the beauty of a leaf, and in the perfection of a dog's ear, and in the kindness in the glance of the mother's eye, my heart is filled with gratitude. That gratitude has to go somewhere. The vessel of my heart is filled, overflowing and spills out into service. So you do not serve to fix things, you serve as a joyful expression of gratitude to your Lord.

If service is done from this point of view, then the service is light, it is gentle and it is unassuming. It does not claim any significance for the server. Service done from any other point of view is poison. It is demeaning both to the server and to the served.

If you should help somebody across the road with a sanctimonious attitude that says; 'Oh, look how good I am, and how useful I am to you', you may just as well have kicked the person because your act has been empty. Your generosity has meant nothing. Your generosity was nothing but a claim to significance.

We know that the only Significant is He. Everything else is a reflection of Him. The essence of shirk is to assign significance to anything other than Him. The worst shirk is for the self to claim significance for itself. That is darkness. We are made to cast the light of our consciousness over the magnificence of His work and to recognize that it is awesome. The two beams in my eyes are like torches that light up that which is out there, that which is a hidden treasure.

However, when I find myself significant these beams no longer shine out to touch the wonder out there, they now flip in. The self tries to make itself seen to itself. The result of this is that nothing is illumined but everything remains in darkness. A person who finds himself significant is repulsive, perverse and ugly. They are misapplying their attention to a purpose that it was not designed for. Your attention is made for Him, not yourself.

Therefore, the secret to achieving success on this path is to first cultivate an attitude of gratitude for that which you have and for what you can see. Look at the things that actually surround you. If you are not amazed by what is around you, you are not seeing it as it is. It is impossible not to find something that is immediately around you, in any given moment, which is not truly astonishing.

Why are your hands shaped like this? Why do you have hard skin under the soles of your feet? Why do you see light and hear sound?

How does your breakfast become your ability to catch the bus? The design of things is truly extraordinary.

Therefore, the gratitude that I am talking about is not what your mother admonished you for. 'Eat your dinner and think about all the starving children in Ethiopia'. It is not like that. It is to open your eyes and to look at what is around you. Is it not amazing? You might be murderously furious with somebody, but if you cannot look at that person and find something quite beautiful about him or her, then you are lying to yourself.

It may be something quite simple. It may be the shape of their jawbone or the shape of their hands. If you observe them carefully there is always disproportionately more in any human being that one can be amazed with than there is to be irritated about. This means that to stay irritated is a choice. It is a choice based on deliberately filtering out that which is amazing.

When you are reacting negatively to a person there is always more to them than what you are reacting to. However, you have to allow your vision to widen so that you can pick up more than the things that you are reacting to. The measure of the degree to which you have done that is the degree to which you can spontaneously and sincerely exclaim *"Al Hamdulillah"* in the situation. You are only seeing this situation as it is while you are truly enchanted and amazed with it. This is what we are taught is bewilderment.

Only based on this fullness of heart can you trust your own action or does your action become trustworthy. When you transact with the world from this place, you are no longer transacting with the world in order to be important, useful or significant. You are transacting with the world in order to express your gratitude to your Lord.

We usually get this the wrong way round. I work in order to achieve something or to get something. You say; 'well what is it that you want?' Then I say 'I want to have peace', or 'I want to have a sense of fulfilment'. This is why I do things. This is why I work. I want to have a full heart. I want to feel secure.

However, this is the wrong way around. You do not have to work to have a grateful heart, you know. Have a grateful heart and then you can work. In fact then only is your work worthy, constructive and of real benefit to yourself and others because then it is worship. It is the other way around. The fulfilment you are after is immediately at hand. You do not work to get happiness. You are happy and therefore you work, as a spontaneous dance of gratitude to your Rabb.

You do not have to look for this, it is with you already. It is closer to you than your jugular vein. Shaykh Fadhlallah once asked me; *"What does asalaamu aleikum, mean?"* I mumbled some nonsense and he replied: *"It means, the peace is already with you."* You do not have to achieve anything. It is here. What are you looking for? You are looking for the thing that you are sitting on. The Vietnamese Zen monk Thich Nhat Hahn expresses this well when he says *"There is no way to enlightenment, enlightenment is the way."*

This means that there is no path to have a quiet heart which is at peace. Have the quiet heart and then you will see the way. Be grateful and you will see what you should do.

It is only once your action is this way around, first the full heart and then the act, that you will stop wanting to manage the affair when you look into the future. You will see that, I have looked at it and I have found His sign. Everything that has come out of the past demonstratively has Allah's signature on it. The tree has it, the car has it, the man's face has it, the event has it and even the person I wanted to throttle has it. They all have it. Subhaanallah!

They all bear this incredible sense of design. Everything has a sense of design. If you look carefully, you will see that even the silliest little events in your life have a design. Initially it seems as though they have no significance at all. However, reflect about it carefully and you will see a pattern. You will see the patterns of meaning that are woven through your life and through the cosmos. In this pattern everything is in place. Nothing is arbitrary. There are no accidents.

Every single event comes from one Hand. There is One Writer to that script, and that is Allah. There is no one other, no one else; there is no other cause. He is the cause. When you know that, it means that when you look into the future you accept that which is coming towards you. It is coming from the same sense of design, and what you then do does not interfere with that sense of design, it helps it. When you are no longer taking charge, your actions are trustworthy. They are trustworthy because you and your interests are not in them.

If your actions towards the world are based on a desire to take charge, you are not acting on why you are here. You are here to witness that He is in charge. He has only made us to know Him. So if you look at what is coming towards you, and you say that you want to stop this or alter it your attitude is consistent with shirk.

It is ignorance. You have missed the point of why you have been created. He is in charge. We are not in charge. He is the Creator, we are the creatures. He is the Puppeteer and we are the puppets. He is the Director and we are the actors. He has written the play and we are the characters.

He is the Author and the only reason He has written all of this, is so that we can appreciate the story. The whole universe that you get presented with is a story that is written for you for one reason only, for your appreciation and delight. That is why He has written it. He has done it all to enchant you.

His creation is therefore the supreme act of love, the supreme manifestation of generosity. He informs us that He has done all of this because He wants to share His wonders. Because, who is He? He is the Hidden Treasure which proclaims 'I love to be known'. He is the Wonderful, He is the Majestic, and that is what He wants to share with you. He grants you your existence from Him so that He can share His with you, so that you may be delighted.

Our job is to be nothing other than an appreciative audience. In addition, while we stay on that path of appreciative gratitude, we are saved. We can then trust our actions. We can know that we will deal with the world correctly. As soon as our perspective moves away from that, and it does not matter how benevolent we are trying to be, or how good, or how kind, our actions are danger ous to ourselves an others.

He is the One who grants sickness, He is the One who grants health. He grants you the capacity to facilitate the help so that you can see the extraordinary nature of His design. Your capacity and your assistance are at best nothing other than instruments that bear witness that His design works. The farmer does not grow the tree, he facilitates the growth. The doctor does not heal the patient, he facilitates healing. Farmers do not make trees and doctors do not make health. These things existed before the farmer or the doctor were there. These things existed in the natural order of things, the natural order decreed by the Lord.

From one point of view we could say that these things only exist to indicate that His machinations work. The healing of the patient and the growing of the tree exist because they provide yet another vantage point from which we may be amazed at Him. This allows one to disconnect from outcomes, and allows one to see the wonder in things that do not apparently go our way.

Thus when the doctor is treating the patient and the patient dies he is still amazed at his Lord. He still sees the design in the apparently dysfunctional.

When we crack this our whole attitude towards existence becomes pleasant, joyful, experimental and curious. It is not heavy and does not presume to carry the burdens of the world or having to fix the world. It is light. Our attitude towards life should be light hearted, kind and appreciative. Not bent with woes and concerns of how terrible things are and how hard we have to work to fix it. It is not up to us to fix it.

He has promised us quite emphatically in the Qur'an that the world and everything in it are not fixable because they are cast in a mould of cataclysmic destruction. There will come a day that He will rip these mountains apart, there will come a day in which He will smash this whole existence to atoms. Al Hamdulillah.

So, stop this silliness of trying to save the world. Save yourselves. Save yourselves by taking on your true status of worshipping. This means you are the one who seeks to be nothing other than grateful, appreciative, and amazed at what is happening. Be the one who is so fascinated with the actions of his Lord that he has a pleasant disregard for the outcomes. Take on the status of the faqir, which is not to wish to be in the sun when you are in the shade and not to wish to be in the shade when you are in the sun.

It is all good and it is all from One Source, and there is no disapproval about it. If you do not have this attitude in this age, you will go mad. There is so much kufr around us, so much mayhem and destruction that it is not possible to stay sane without this attitude. We are going into what is probably the one of the biggest financial collapses of the last two hundred years. It will equal the depression of the Thirties and more.

The global economic markets will fall apart.

If you cannot wash your hands of the affair, if you cannot say that this is not my affair but His affair, the mayhem will squash you. If you have a vested interest in the outcome you will not be of those who witness that what is happening now is the natural balancing of the imbalance caused by the unbridled greed of the age. You will not be of those reading the book; you will be one of the characters in the plot, the plot of self-destruction.

Be the spectator, do not be the fixer. Paradoxically, when you get this right what you do will in fact help to fix things profoundly, because when you act what you do is precise, and surgical because you are His instrument. Then He can use you, because you are not involved. You see, that while you are trying to fix the thing, your nafs is involved. It is your own idea of what needs to happen.

However, if you give up trying to be in charge of the thing and your heart is moved to do something, you can do it unconditionally. He then acts through you. Then that one act is worth a thousand acts. That one act is like removing the single brick that causes the entire building to collapse. You have an efficiency of action when you have this approach, because it is not you who throws, it is Allah who throws!

———

May Allah grant us success on the path.

May He grant us nearest to Him.

May He grant us annihilation in Him.

Allah, grant peace and blessings on our Nabi (s.a.w.s.)

Al Hamdulillah.

The Worship of the Free
Discourse 9: 26th April, 2001

Bismillahir Rahmanir Rahim:

"La illaha ill Allah" There is no being who is worthy of worship other than Allah. That which is worshipped is that which is truly significant, truly meaningful and worthy of attention, praise and awe. So, there is none significant other than Allah. There is no other source of meaning other than Allah. There is none of consequence other than Allah.

La illaha ill Allah means more than a simple statement that there is no other god but God. This is a flat translation. La illaha ill Allah means that there is nothing that is worthy of being granted awe and therefore significance, other than Allah. When you see it from that point of view, it becomes abundantly clear that although one may be a Muslim and maybe a person who has proclaimed the shahada it does not mean that one is free of idolatry, of shirk. All of us have our own projects in mind. We have our own ideas of what is significant and we construct our lives around these things. This person thinks that it is important to become wealthy and he therefore grants significance to wealth. In so far as he grants significance to wealth, he commits shirk.

The next person thinks that it is significant and important to be piling up good deeds for akhira, (the hereafter). This person is worshipping the garden; and so they are also guilty of shirk. Although their action is less conditional in so far as they are not trying to benefit themselves immediately, they are still pursuing an outcome, which is to win the delights of the garden.

The third person considers that the whole purpose of existence, the whole reason he or she is here, is to worship Allah. That person is the pinnacle of creation. That person is the person for whom the whole of creation has been made.

Shaykh Ali Al Jamal distinguishes between three categories of people. He says there are the bondsmen, who are the people who want to get things out of this life. They are trapped. They have no freedom, because their state of being is defined by this world. Then he says there are the hirelings. Those people are in this world in order to earn the favour of Allah so that they may gain Paradise.

So they are doing their good deeds in order to please Allah in order to gain Paradise. So it is still a conditional motive. In addition, there is a level of shirk in this, because the concern of a person like this is that they are in a negotiation with Allah. They are trying to win their good fortune and their good auspices from Allah by paying the price that they think Allah has asked of them.

Thirdly you get those people who are truly free. They do not have the slightest concern for either this world or the hereafter. They are not concerned about paradise; they are only concerned about their Lord. They are concerned with being in awe of the Creator of it all. It is only this person who understands that the whole purpose of existence is to be in awe. It is only this person who can at all be considered fully human. It is only this person who can be considered to be a believer.

All other modes of belief are conditional. They are limited and they are weak. In all other aspects of belief you still find conditional thinking. You find an element of wanting to manage the affair. Managing your own affair assumes that you can manipulate a set of conditions that will have a beneficial outcome to you.

The most primitive and immature way of doing that is to think that you can manipulate a set of conditions that will have a beneficial outcome for you in this life. The next set of conditions is concerned with manipulating events in order to get a beneficial outcome for yourself in the next life. All of these are still putting yourself in charge of your own affair. We want to make a success of this matter, of how we understand existence. In the process we forget that our true success lies in Islam.

Islam means submission; it means to give up, to disallow any pretence of being of any use to yourself or being of any use to others. It means to root out the ignorant hope that you can manipulate a set of conditions that are beneficial to your desired outcome or to yourself. Your benefit is not in your hands; your benefit is in His hands.

Your good auspices are not with you, they are with Him. If He chooses for you the blessing the weight of a mustard seed, an army of a hundred thousand cannot take it from you. If He wishes for you a curse the size of a pin, a whole army of angels will not protect you. He is the One who is managing the affair. In addition, the reason why He made us is to witness that this is the case.

In order for us to discover that is the case, He has made us in such a way that we will attempt to come to our own defence and fail. We have to fail at being in charge ourselves. We have to earn the bitter fruit of thinking that we can be of any use to ourselves in this life or the next before we let go of the reins.

Allah presents us with challenges all the time. That challenge really asks us; 'Whom are you putting in charge? Yourself ? Or are you really relying on Me? Are you going to leap into the abyss or are you going to stick to the safe, the known and predictable that you have worked out for yourself ?' Repeatedly in our life- time we come to crossroads, we come to points where we know in the depths of our hearts, that the next step forward, requires a leap; a leap into the abyss, a leap into the unknown. We do not know what the next day will bring. Those leaps are leaps of faith.

What is faith? Faith is the capacity to convince yourself that He is in charge. Faith is the capacity to silence your inner dialogue. Your inner dialogue is all about keeping yourself busy with your own agenda. Keeping yourself focused on the set of events and actions which you think will have an outcome that will be beneficial to you. It is consistently appraising the things that you do on the basis of the benefits coming to you and to be chatting away to yourself all the time, about the best way to get what you want.

Imaan or belief suggests that you have stopped this silly pre-occupation because you understand that you can not do your- self any good. You have stopped trying to work the matter out. You have stopped trying to have a hold on existence, to bend it to your will. Instead, you have started to appreciate it. You have started to witness it and to be in awe of it; to see that its design is fundamentally benevolent towards you.

So when we are playing it safe, we are trying to steer on the side of reasonableness and of being in charge of our lives. In reality, what we are actually doing is denying His Absoluteness. We are behaving as if He is not in charge. This is particularly true in situations where our hearts are quickened, where our being tells us move, but on the basis of our biographical entrapment, we do not move.

All of us have experienced this in the path, it is common, and we all get these moments. We all face things which stimulate our curiosity but which we refrain from pursuing because we are too busy being 'good' or 'responsible'.

The depressing thing is that when you do not move, the same crossroad has a sneaky way of coming back to you. The second time it is visited onto you, it is visited on you in such a way that it is far less avoidable and far more insistent. Each time it intensifies it causes you far more distress. In other words, if you do not leap off the cliff, you will be tossed off it.

We have within us two potentials. One is of bondage, of mediocrity and of grey depression. The other is to be an enchanted ecstatic on our journey of discovery. We choose either one or the other. There is no such thing as a human being that does not have the capacity to be a complete monster or to rise higher than the angels. We all have the same range of possibility.

Being a monster is concerned with trying to bend existence to our will; that is, trying to make existence deliver to us that which we want. By doing that, we are denying three things. Firstly, that existence has a design to it. Secondly, that that design is bigger than we are. Thirdly, that the design has more to offer us than we can offer ourselves and is fundamentally benevolently disposed to- wards us. It has our best interests at heart, even more than we have. You cannot do better for yourself than what Allah is going to do for you.

The degree to which you try to manage your affair is the degree to which He leaves you to manage that affair. It is therefore also the degree to which you will mess things up. You will settle for the second best, for that which is drab, mediocre, depressing and dispirited.

The degree to which you accept whatever He puts in front of you; whatever He quickens your heart with, is the degree to which you allow Him to determine the outcome. He promises us that if we follow the quickening of our hearts, He will only give us better. This is His promise.

It is how He has created existence. He is the Beneficent, He is the Sustainer, He is the Provider, He is the Overflowing, and He has no limitations.

So, rest in those Hands. Allow yourself to fall back into that security. The only other alternative is to collapse into the insecurity of your ingenuity and what you then have is your own delusion. It is your own mirage that looks as though it is going to work at first, but instead fails you miserably.

21

All of us are designed to be fundamentally uneasy with the mediocrity of our day to day existence. It is precisely that dis- ease which causes us to leap forward, to seek out the high. Some of us spend our whole lives lying to ourselves about our essential aloneness and unhappiness with this mediocrity. The rest of us get fed up with suffering and commit to the path.

_____

May Allah grant us success on the path.

May He grant us nearness to Him.

May He grant us annihilation in Him.

May Allah, grant peace and blessings on our blessed. Nabi (s.a.w.s.)

Al Hamdulillah.

_____

21: For an overview of the Qur'anic perspective on this please see [6:95-108], particularly verse's 107-108: _"If it had been Allah's plan, they would not have taken false gods, but we made you not one to watch over their doings, nor are you set over them to dispose of their affairs. Revile not ye those whom they call upon besides Allah, lest they out of spite revile Allah in their ignorance. Thus have we made alluring to each people their doings. In the end will they return to their Lord, and We shall then tell them the truth of all that they did."_

Journeying through the Three Stations
Discourse 10: 18th May, 2001

Bismillahir Rahmanir Rahim:

Shaykh Ibn Ajiba describes three stations on the path. He says that the first station is the station of the contracting employee with the contractor. For many of us our station with Allah is like that. We have a clearly set out idea of our obligations against the contract and also a clearly set out idea of the punishments and the consequences that will follow if we do not act in terms of the contract.

In this case, our view of Allah is a vision of law; it is an image that has within it elements of the judgmental father; the One who is critical and who is weighing every action. This means that we start off on the path with trying to be careful, by wanting to do the right thing. Our attitude is the attitude of a person who thinks 'If I do the right thing and walk my shoes straight, then Allah will give me my just reward.'**22**

So we assume a negotiating position with regard to Allah. This is the attitude of a contracting employee, the one who is still negotiating and haggling; that is, the one who still has a measure of choice. Mercifully, as we grow with the path, this station does not last because it is a very difficult station to be in. It is a place of great discomfort. It is a place of being constantly fearful and disapproving, precisely because you feel that you are being judged and disapproved of all the time. This station is only appropriate for a person to have in their youth, when their riotous passions are still likely to get them into trouble.

However, Shaykh Ibn Ajiba points out that as we mature in Allah, our station becomes much more like a child with its mother. Allah becomes the One we call on all the time. When we are perplexed, we share it with

Him; 'Allah, what is this? Please help me.' When we are happy we share that happiness with Him. Subhaanallah. When we are sad we take our tears to Him. When we are confused we lift our hands up to Him. When we are anxious we take protection and succour in Him. It is the station of the child with its mother. It is the station of the one who still has independent will, but he is no longer arguing with the contractor because it is the station of the child who is convinced of the love of the mother.

So we shift our attitude towards Allah from that of a judgmental paternal figure or being, to that of a nurturing maternal presence. One that is here, One that has an interest, One Whom we can truly take our problems, our suffering and all our joys to. The quality of the salah of the person who is in this state is far different from the quality of the salah of a person who is in the state of the contracting employee. If you are in the subcontracting position, you will experience your 'salah' as hard work. It will be onerous, it will be a job that you have to do, and it is an obligation that needs to be completed. Your experience of the fardh will be quite literally the obligatory. There will be no pleasure and joy in it, you do it because you have to do it.

So, you will do everything that you have to do, but you will do it with the attitude of a bondsman, with a slight sense of resignation and compulsion in it. However as you mature on the path, your conversation, your salah becomes a conversation with Allah. It is not something that you do because it has to be done. It is longer something that becomes onerous, something that is a difficult burden. It becomes a place where you have some quiet and peace.

Imagine the child having played in the garden for a long time and having cut and bruised himself. Suddenly this child comes into the house, sees its mother and then runs over to the mother for a cuddle, attention and soothing. This is how we experience our salah in this second station. You have been out into the world, you have been trading, you have been arguing, you have been working, it has been very difficult and you come to your salah with the attitude of 'I am coming home to mother, I am coming home to that which embraces and which enfolds me and gives me quiet.'

Make no mistake. The second state will not happen if you did not come through the door of the first state. Do not think that you can get into the throne-room without walking through the gates of the palace. You have got to pay your dues. You have got to start walking the path. Walking the path is literally by faith. It means that you do not know, that you are not seeing, you have not experienced that quiet, you have not experienced that peace. And yet, you trust that one day it will be there. However, at first you will bow your head because you are commanded to do so and for no other reason.

Without the hard work at the outset, without being in the position of the contracted employee, you cannot earn the station of the child with its mother. However in terms of the description Shaykh Ibn Ajiba gives, even this second station is not permanent, nor is it the ultimate. This station still means that, like the child going out into the garden, you have the assumption that there are patches of time when you are free to pursue your own thing.

Between your salah and your ibada, there is still 'you in the world', you with your family, you pursuing your career, you doing your own thing. After this there is ibada and salah, the time with your Lord. Your worship therefore is not a twenty-four hour fascination.

This station has therefore its own weakness, and its weak- ness is confusion. This weakness is concerned with the fact that you keep getting yourself into trouble. You keep on forgetting and so soon after remembering the peace of the embrace of the salah, you are distracted in the games of the world so that you have to remember once again. You keep on forgetting and remembering, in cycles of trouble and peace. You get bruised, perplexed and con- fused so you end up having to go back to mother, only to rush out again for another cycle of suffering and disquiet.

So there comes the challenge to take the state of peace that you have in your salah into your daily life. I once had a discussion with Shaykh Fadhlallah about a khalwa I was about to do. He instructed me to go and speak to Shaykh Asaf about the khalwa. I knew Shaykh Asaf was very strict regarding this sort of thing so I had some trepidation about speaking to him. Some days later I had a conversation with Shaykh Asaf.

Shaykh Asaf wanted to know if I slept in khalwa and I said; *"Yes, Shaykh Asaf"* and then he said: *"Well, don't!"* and of course I was horrified. Khalwa is tough enough, and the thought of not being permitted to sleep at all filled me with horror. So I went back to Shaykh Fadhlallah and I said; *"You know, Shaykh Asaf says that I should not sleep in the khalwa."* Shaykh

Fadhlallah replied *"Well, do not take him too seriously. Shaykh Asaf is in khalwa all the time."*

Shaykh Fadhlallah's view was that Shaykh Asaf was at such an elevated station that he was in khalwa all the time. What does being in the khalwa mean? If nothing else, khalwa means to be in a state of intense worship, like a very long salah. So Shaykh Asaf was in khalwa all the time. He was in that state of intensity 24 hours out of every 24.

This means that what he experienced was not just a special time; it was not a separate event or a separate moment. It was the ground state of his being. This state of continuous worship, of continuous connectedness to the Lord is what Shaykh Ibn Ajiba describes as the station of the corpse in the hands of the washer. (This description has had some misuse amongst the Sufi's).**23**

It originally described the state of a person in baqa, the station of 'going on by Allah', because it is the state of a person who no longer has any independent will whatsoever. His hand only moves if it is moved by Allah. His foot only moves if it is moved by Allah. He has no will of his own. It is not like the child who runs away from the mother and then gets hurt and then runs back to mother. 'Mother' is inescapable. Allah is inescapable. There is no place to hide. Wherever you turn, there is the face of Allah. You have no choice. You have no volition.

Shaykh al Akbar, Ibn Arabi described this state by saying that some of the greatest works that he wrote he did not know what he would write a minute before he wrote it. He was completely not himself. He was not there. He did not act, he did not think about his act before he acted. He did not know what he was going to say before he said it.**24**

What an incredible thing to say. Here is this most incredibly eloquent man, one of the greatest lights of tasawwuf, a man who spanned the whole of the Islamic world. He taught from Seville to Damascus. He would have thousands listening to him. He himself said; 'I do not know what I am going to say until I start saying it.' He would not think about an argument, he would not discuss, he would not develop a discourse.

He would move his lips and Allah would make the speech. In this station you have no voli tion of your own.

There is a parallel between these three phases and the phases of journeying which you have probably heard before. They are hearing, seeing and being. It is said that the journey starts when you start hearing accounts or stories that there is a 'fire' in the for- est. As a young man you hear about these amazing people who do these extraordinary things. All you know is that these people are called sufi's, and they are instructed by these rather strange men called shaykh's.

It all sounds a bit odd and kind of enchanting, but you keep busy with your life. You are trying to get married and settle down, getting a job and making a success of it all. You hear of them and it is sort of interesting. That is the first station. This is the station of the contracted bondsman, this station of hearing that there is a fire in the forest. Like all bondsmen you dutifully start walking in that direction prescribed for you. You are now paying your dues, doing your time in this world, and pursuing your aims in this world.

Then the terrain changes because this story that you have heard turns out not to be a story. It is no longer a story, because you begin to see the fire in the forest. Every so often when you are at an elevated place on the path, you see the unmistakable glow of fire on the horizon. This is the station of the one who is like the child with its mother. You start having these odd experiences, after dhikr or after salah. You experience an incredible peace and quiet, happiness like you cannot describe.

Although you may have wanted to throttle your wife just before, or shoot your boss; or your child upsets you terribly, or whatever; you have these moments. In a very dark and stormy landscape there is a sudden break in the clouds and a sharp burst of sunlight lights everything up. So you have patches where you start experiencing things very differently. This is seeing fire in the forest. You get evidence that the story that you have been following had some reality to it. It was not just a story. It is not just information anymore. It is not just words anymore. It is not what comes out of a text. You are like the person who has only read about lions suddenly coming across lion tracks in his back garden.

One of the attributes of this station is that you have in- stances of things that you cannot explain rationally. You start seeing things in your everyday life that you can only account for on the basis of divine intervention. You begin to witness the acts of Allah in your day to day life. You witness his acts in others' lives. You meet an extraordinary shaykh or you read an account of the Prophet (s.a.w.s.). Suddenly you don't experience it as a kind of fairy tale. At first when you read the account of these extraordinary beings, it was as if they were from a kind of fairyland. It was a different time, in a different place. All disconnected; nothing to do with me.

But then things change, because you start seeing intervention in your life. You start seeing things that you cannot account for. It may start very innocently, for example at a meeting or a discussion that you have. Today you have never heard of a particular subject, it is the first time that you heard of this subject, and soon after, you see a book, or you read a newsmagazine article about it. You meet someone who explains that this phenomenon is called synchronicity, yet another thing you have never heard of.

After a while it occurs to you that these patterns are some- how connected to you. You have an increasing conviction that Allah is engaging you in a conversation and He is using events as His words. There is meaning coming to you from the world around you. This is not just a set of accidents. It is seeing the fire in the forest. Then these patches of seeing grow. 25 It is not just a little patch of sunlight here and a little patch of sunlight there. You start realizing that from the moment you wake up to the moment that you go to bed, He was talking to you every single step of the way. He is in front of you, He is behind you. He was the One who caused that woman to cross your path and look at you in a way that upset you. He was the One who made the cat to sit on your lap so that you could have some kindness and quietness. He was the One that brought the child with the cup of tea when you were about to throttle that person over there. He brings it all. And you find no escape. That is when you become the fire in the forest. He is wherever you turn, not as a statement of belief, but as a first hand experienced truth. Wherever you turn, there is the One Reality. It is inescapable.

So in the course of this journey your character changes. These three perceptions; the hearing of the fire in the forest, the seeing of the fire in the forest, the becoming of the fire in the for- est are not the same.

The station of the contracted employee, the station of the child with its mother and the station of the corpse in the hands of its washer are not the same.

Your character changes and you will see yourself changing as you see other people change as they go on the path. At first you are very disapproving of everyone and everything else. It's a struggle and no fun; always the sour face; always disapproving. This changes, (your brothers hopefully should not have to wait too long), because as you become like the child with its mother, your character changes accordingly. It becomes somewhat naïve and a little bit bewildered. You get easily knocked off balance. You more and more frequently bump into these disturbances, and realise you cannot make it all work. You often feel out of control.

Although you were very serious and thought you were in charge you discovered you were not in charge. You were working so hard to make it all happen, for your life to succeed, and just when you thought it was going to succeed and that you have got it all right the whole thing collapsed. For example, you have got this wonderful business and you have it all worked out right and then your partner runs away with all the money. He goes to Pakistan. It's inexplicable!

This way of looking at life, thinking you can make it work, control it, will ultimately fail. You may consider this failure as paying your dues. But at some point you realize that you cannot pay your dues. How do you pay your dues to Allah? How do you repay the genius and the intelligence behind the design of your left lung? You could work for a thousand years and yet still not repay that. If you had to get somebody to actually go and design all the little bits and pieces that go into making your life, get a thousand engineers to work together for two centuries, they could not get it right.

It is impossible to repay. It is impossible to pay your dues. So you realize that every time you think that you are going to pay them, you cause trouble. The trouble that you are causing yourself is basically based on arrogance. Look who you are trying to negotiate with. You cannot negotiate with Allah. Who are you having an argument with? Subhaanallah.

So, over time, your character becomes less negotiating, less disapproving and less insistent on doing the right thing. You become more interested in why you cannot make things work. It perplexes you, and your salah takes on a different character. When you are going to salah it is like the child running back to its mother. 'Allahu Akbar. It has been hell out there this afternoon, I mean, I did this negotiating, I tried to do a piece of work with that person and it was a disaster. On the other hand this person came out of nowhere and gave me something, I did not earn it, I did not do anything for it, and I do not understand.'

In other words, you get taken into an embrace, and the embrace says; 'You do not need to understand. You are not in charge, you have given up, you are in submission, and you are in Islam.' And so your character is sweeter, is less disapproving, and less confused.

This is the station of the elite. In western tasawwuf we are also familiar with these categories. These categories refer to the difference between the common, the elite and the elite of the elite. The common are those who are still busy with the contract. The elite are those who are perplexed, who just want to get off this treadmill of running this contract. Then you get the elite of the elite, those who are colourless, who are neither bewildered nor hardworking. They have no character, other than what Allah puts in them at that point in time.

These people can then come back into the world and be useful to others. The people in the middle are somewhat dangerous because they cannot really be trusted. They cannot be trusted not because they are dishonest, but because they know that the contract does not work. They are therefore somewhat unpredictable.

They are people of wandering and wayfaring. They are not committed to one place. They are not committed to building a future anymore. They have become fed up with their future.

_____

May Allah grant us freedom from our own fear.
May Allah make us aware of Him as our constant Companion.
May He make us companionable with Him.
May Allah grant us conversation with Him and comfort in Him.
May Allah grant us a gentle hand with the world around us.
May Allah grant us a just hand with the world around us.
May Allah grant us nearness to him.
May Allah grant us annihilation.
May Allah grant us death before we die.

Al Hamdulillah

_____

22: For example, this is like Elizabeth Kubler Ross's third stage of grief - bargaining in the face of death.

23: A.A. - This description of the corpsein the hands of the washer has been grosslymisused by certain so-called Sufi masters who use it as a means to manipulate their mureed's; emotionally, spiritually and physically.

24: A.A. - Shaykh al-Akbar gives another superb metaphor for this state; to be 'like a stone that falls where it is thrown.

25: 'Witnessing.'

SHIFTING PERCEPTION: SHIFTING THE WORLDVIEW
Discourse 11: 6th June, 2001

Bismillahir Rahmanir Rahim:

Allah created existence because He loved to be known. We do not read and we are not taught that He hated not to be known. We are taught that He loved to be known. The significance of this is that existence commences with and is concerned with affirmation and not negation. Existence is about YES and not about NO. From one point of view the state of love or attraction and the state of hate or repulsion are the same because they both precipitate movement. Love or attraction pulls towards and hate or repulsion pushes away from, both are catalysts of movement.

If we understand that the first principle of all existence is a principal attraction, of love, it means that a negating demeanour is fundamentally misguided and misguiding. It suggests that the principle of existence is the principle of love. And to allow yourself to be drawn towards, to swoon, to be enchanted with, to be attracted to, is all part of the same affair of discovering your nature. The essential nature that underlines all existence is a great resounding affirmation, a great YES.

This means that we have to be very circumspect about our 'nay' saying capacity. We must be careful of how easily we wield the sword of separation and of negation. We do this much too easily, we are awfully opinionated. We look at somebody and we say; 'Oh, he is such and such, and that person is so and so, and that person does this, and that person is not really a Muslim because he has this peculiar view in his fiqh, and that person is like that, and this person is like this'.

In the process we are not just cutting that person. Understand, a cut against existence is a cut against yourself, because the cut of alienating existence is the cut of alienating yourself. It is the cut of repulsion. Continued repulsion only leads you into complete isolation, separation and loneliness. If you keep on moving away, you eventually move away from all that can be moved away from and then there is nothing left.

You find yourself miserable, sour, opinionated and despised, rejected by people, with no love. But if you soften your heart and allow yourself to be enchanted with that which is affirmable in the people around you, (and make no mistake, everybody has something that you can affirm), your heart goes towards that which attracts, draws forward; not that which repels.

This drawing forward delivers you to the opposite place of the place of alienation. It delivers you to a place of affirmation. A place of homecoming; a place of connectedness with the whole of existence. You are at the centre and not at the periphery. Continuous negation and continuous pushing away delivers you to a point of the absolutely peripheral, complete negation. Affirmation, the path of love, is the path that we are on, and the 'Deen' is a path of love. The story of the Rasul (s.a.w.s.) is a story of love. All of the shaykh's are concerned with love. The whole matter is an issue of intoxication and of love.

To continuously swoon, to be amazed at, to be enchanted with, and to be attracted, delivers you to the source of attraction, it delivers you to the centre. Negating delivers you to the periphery. Affirming and going towards, delivers you to the centre.

Now, any moment can be seen from one or the other perspective. You could say that I am working hard at this job because I hate being poor. That is seeing the work from the perspective of repulsion. Or you could say that I am working hard at this job because I love to work, to make a useful contribution. Both are equally possible, and the movement that comes from each is equally true. However, one movement has at its source fear, and the other movement has at its source affirmation. What we find is that as we progress on the path less and less of our own motive is based on fear and more and more of it is based on affirmation. You no longer do your salah because you are terrified of getting it wrong and ending up in the place where you do not want to be when you die.

You start doing your salah because you love doing it, because you love to draw near. You do not fast because it is merely prescribed, and that if you do not do it, you call upon yourself the disapproval and the hatred of Allah. You fast because you love to fast. So, as you journey on this path you more and more construct your motive around attraction and around affirmation. When you start doing that you find that you become a being that is quite different from most other people, because you literally stop turning your world on its head. You start inverting the pattern of perception.

Most people construct their lives around insecurities or fears, around repulsion, rather than around attraction. When the man goes to work, the reason why he goes to work is not because he is attracted by the work, but because he is fleeing the possible state of impoverishment. He believes that he is going to be impoverished if he does not work. The man comes home and smiles at his wife, not because he loves to smile at his wife or is pleased to see her but because he thinks that if he does not smile at his wife, his life will become unliveable.

So we do something not because we love to do it or because we are attracted to it, but we do it because we are frightened, we are trying to avoid the consequence of not doing it. Most adult people are like this. They are people of avoidance, people of repulsion, of negation. Very little of what they do is done for the love of doing it. Most things that are done are seen as the necessary price that has to be paid to earn the few pleasures either of this life or the hereafter.

Whereas, the path that we are on is a path that cultivates the habit of pleasure and of enjoyment and of taking delight in what you are doing now, knowing full well that when you act from this intent that your Lord will also reward you incalculably from His treasure trove. Delight upon delight. In this state, you have about yourself an air of delighted curiosity, knowing that it would be wonderful and that you cannot wait to see it. And in fact it is wonderful precisely because you do not understand what it is going to be. So, you are not pushed away from and defined by the fear, but rather, you are being drawn toward, out of innocence and a curiosity about the existence, because you want to affirm it.

So, this way of looking is the opposite of the way of looking which makes the current world view work. The current world view expects adults to be brave, depressed, miserable, cheerless, loveless, lonely and discontented. It functions on these people. It requires that state for it to run. Whereas the beings that come out of the circle are exactly the opposite. They are curious, delighted, delighting, delightful, affirming, kind, trusting and loving. These are different people from the average people we find today. What makes them different is that they literally invert how the perception of the conventional person works.

You see, by affirming, you are not wishing to be affirmed. Wishing to be affirmed means that you create the condition where the other has power over you. And that gathers you to the other (creates a dependence on the other).

Shaykh Ali Al Jamal says that if you are outwardly gathered, you will be inwardly separate, and if you are inwardly gathered, you will be outwardly separate. If you want something from somebody else, that person's ability to withhold what you want makes you manipulable; it gives him or her power over you.

In other words, while you want something, your being is held in the clutches of the other. You become peripheral, you become defined, you become weak, and you are not at centre. On the other hand, if you focus on what you should be contributing, you go back to centre. Contribution is, by definition, affirmation. Contribution means, I am not here to negate you, or to get something from you. It means rather that I am here to affirm you, to give you something. I am here to assist you. You are worthy of my care, my love and my regard.

Giving or taking patterns in one of two ways. Fundamentally it either has to do with things or it has to do with significance. A person who is here to make a contribution, or to give to life, finds the other significant. He is not wishing to gain significance from the other. He is not negating the other. He is affirming the other. He says that the other is significant. He is here to give.

That status of being, of granting significance to the other, is the position of the humble one who always says yes and has a kind face. That is the person who goes into the centre of the affair. That is the person who ultimately defines the outcome of events, because this is a person who is working with the fundamental direction and impetus of the decree.

The decree is, by definition, things as they are presented to you in the moment that you are in.26 The decree is Allah speaking to you. To negate what is presented to you is to negate Him. Islam means submission. It means to submit to what has been decreed and to affirm it. To become it's ally. To become the ally of what is, means to solicit the support of all things. It therefore means the one who submits becomes inexplicably influential. He is at centre, not peripheral. When you serve the other that is presented to you, you befriend it, and by befriending it you become the khalifa - the custodian of existence.

Allah did not create for any reason other than His love to be known. Which means, rather than having the status of most people today, who feel that they are weak, who fear that they are peripheral, who fear that they are just in bondage and that they have no power over their lives, you become a person who senses the absolute magnitude and significance of the world that you are in, and the graced status you have as the one who is epicentral to it all.27

You are at the source of the existence which surrounds you. You are at the well. One of the things that you discover is that the dream is the objective world and that reality is the subjective world. It is exactly the opposite of what we think. The realm of the metaphor, the illusion and the allegory is in the objective, material existence.

For instance, if you explore the idea of space, and the limitlessness of space, we have access to two terrains where we can explore the theme of the infinite, and the limitlessness. One is to consider infinity from the point of view of space stretching out in either direction from you. Straight in front of you, going into an unlimited measure, space stretches out from you, to infinity. There will always be another kilometre after the one you have measured. However, as soon as you think of it like that, you are actually thinking of limitlessness by way of space, which is by definition limited. It is like saying; a limitless number of limitations. In other words, space is a metaphor for limitlessness. If you sit for long enough in the silence behind your eyes, and you sink back into the abyss which is at the back of your being, you start to discover that that pit is fundamentally fathomless. It is truly infinite and it has no space. It is not an infinite number of units of measure, metres or kilometres or whatever. It is infinite without measure.

It is infinity contained within a dot, the dot of your consciousness. It is more infinite than objective infinity.

The objective infinity is the metaphor. The real infinity sits behind your eyes. Another way you can see this is to begin to perceive that you are not in the world, it is in you, (this again is not just a metaphor, it becomes a real experience). Most of us have the sense that the other wraps around us. That the rest of the world, the rest of the universe completely encapsulates us and we are in the middle. You point to the 360 degrees around you, 'that is where it is, that is where it is' and so on.

We feel that we are small and that this vastness wraps around us. However, in order to have this perception of the world, you have to involve a third person's point of view. In fact this perception of the world is only possible through the vehicle of language, because as you sit there you do not see or perceive what is behind you; you only perceive what is in front of you. So you have to speculate, you have to create an imagination of what is behind you.**28** The idea that the rest of existence encapsulates you, half of it sitting behind you is purely just an idea. This is not how your perception actually works.

If you consider how your perception actually works, a useful place to start is to look at how vision works, because vision is a very powerful sense in people. For most of us it is our principal sense. If you open your eyes and look in front of you and pay attention to the periphery of your vision, you will be able to identify a clear border which is outlined by a circle in front of you. In front of this border is the seen, and behind this border sits you, the seer.

If you pay attention to the character of this circle of the seen it becomes apparent that it has depth. It is like a bubble. All that you perceive is in that bubble and the perceiver, the looker, is outside that bubble looking in. In other words, perception does not wrap around you, it presents itself in front of you as a bubble. That perception is not just perception by the eye, all perception works like that. We are all witness to every single impulse that comes in the front of our being. All our experience, both audial and visual, is presented in front of our being.

Allowing yourself to slip a little further back into the abyss, where the seeing happens from, means you give up your neediness for the other. This is because when you give up your need, you disconnect from being sucked into the world of the seen, (or bubble). When you stand outside the bub- ble you start to see it as it is. It is like a sphere and the perceiver (you), is this fathomless being that wraps around the bubble. This means that you are on the furthest side of the most distant horizon that you can look out on. It means that the whole of existence is inside you and you wrap around it. So, you are not encapsulated by existence, you encapsulate existence. And what a difference between the person who thinks he is in the world and the person who knows the world is in him.

The person who thinks that he is in the world is a person under threat; he has this vastness, this weight, this infinity on top of him, crushing him. In the face of this danger he is fundamentally and irrevocably vulnerable. He is weakness in essence.

When you are gathered to the other and you experience the self to be encapsulated by the other, you become this tiny be- ing with the rest of infinity wrapped around you, just waiting to crush you out of existence. So, your way of being becomes a way of negation. Fear becomes your way of being. You spend your life running, fleeing from existence.

The person who starts to discover that existence is inside of them, can afford to be enchanted by the **bubble**. They can afford to find it interesting

---

Metamorphosis

I have discovered that my birth lies before me.
In my final moment
all that is my promise will fructify,
then only will all that is me be.

So too my death lies behind me since my past is the ancestor of my present and who I was had to make way for who I am.

I now know that death is not contrary to life, rather, I live in a moment pinned between birth and death and in every instant I die and am born a little.

How sweet this is to know
that my grave is the gateway
of departure and therefore commencement,
the place of the cessation of all hostilities,
of surrender and triumph and attainment of boundlessness within.

Without the world is a metaphor that stretches from me to infinity,
immeasurable measurability.
Within the limitlessness is without measure.

and unthreatening. They are not the small encapsulated by the huge, they are the fathomless totality of the self that encapsulates the other.

———

May Allah grant us freedom from our own fear.

May Allah make us aware of Him as our constant Companion.

May He make us companionable with Him.

May Allah grant us conversation with Him and comfort in Him.

May Allah grant us a gentle hand with the world around us.

May Allah grant us a just hand with the world around us.

May Allah grant us nearness to him.

May Allah grant us annihilation.

May Allah grant us death before we die.

Al Hamdulillah.

———

26: F.A. - The Qur'an: *"To each is a goal to which Allah turns him; then strive together towardsall that is good."* [2:148].

27: F.A. - You becomethis being without presumption - with humility.

28: T.S. - See D. E. Harding's 'On Having no Head.' for more on this subject.

Being Present in the Moment
Discourse 12: 16th February, 2001

Bismillahir Rahmanir Rahim:

Our lives are a succession of periods or epochs. We can measure our lives in years. One year is followed by the next year, which is followed by the next year. However, sooner or later the year that you are in will not have a year behind it. It will be your last year. You have no guarantee that that year is not the year that you are in now. So too our lives are a succession of months, of one month followed by another month, followed by yet another month, and likewise, you have no guarantee that the month which you are in, has a month behind it. You do not know whether right now is not the last month of your life. In a similar vein our lives are a succession of weeks, the one week followed by another week, followed by yet another week, and who is to say that the week which you are in right now has a week behind it? For all you know, this is your last week.

In the same vein our lives are a succession of days, one day followed by another day, and yet another, and who is to say that the day which you are in right now, is going to have another day following it? For all you know, this is the last day of your life. In exactly the same sense your life is a succession of hours, of one hour followed by another hour, followed by yet another hour, and who is to say that the hour which you are in right now, has another hour after it? You cannot say. So, for all you know, you are in the last 60 minutes of your life. In the very same way your life is a succession of moments, of one moment to another moment, followed by yet another moment, and who is to say that the moment you are in right now is going to have a moment after it? You cannot say. All that you can be sure of is the moment that you are in right now.

Right now this building could collapse and kill all of us in an instant. The people who were recently killed in the earthquake in Central America must have been sitting inside, probably having tea or they were talking to their friends, then the world shrugged a little and they were obliterated.

It is vitally important that we take our death as our advisor, because taking your death as your advisor, means understand ing its proximity. It is not an abstract thing; it is not just a thing that happens to other people. It is not a sanitized thing taken care of by undertakers. It is your constant companion; it is only ever one moment away. Sooner or later that moment that you are in is not going to have a moment behind it. You have no guarantee that it is not the moment which you are standing in right now. Death is one moment away. It is terribly immediate and absolutely proximate.

We have this illusion of solidity about our lives. My life presents itself like a building. It is a thing that has stood and will withstand. What an illusion. I am suspended by the nose on the thread of a single breath. Shut it off for a few minutes and I am dead. My entire life hangs by the thread of a single breath. How insubstantial is that?

Now, when one bears that in mind, it becomes also immediately apparent that everything that I do for my own benefit is fundamentally futile. Our managing of events in order to ensure outcomes beneficial to ourselves, our engineering of life, our pulling the strings to deliver only fruit that will delight us, must deliver us to an unsatisfying conclusion. If my life is all about a journey to my benefit and my happiness, then I am living in the land of the inescapable highway robber called Death. At some point he will raid me on one of my journeys to happiness and I will be cut off in mid stride, my feet still attempting to move from the now of discontentment to the then of achievement. My body and my being will be left on the road of desolation without having achieved the journey's end of arrival, of fulfilment and satisfaction. My life made meaningless.

And, strangely, this is also true for those whose intention is purely for Akhira. When we do things for the benefit of the rewards of the Garden, then we assume that we can negotiate our place in Jannat with Allah. This is the most unspeakable arrogance and presumption.

Who do you think you are negotiating with? On what basis do you propose to lay a claim against Him, who gave you the very tongue to articulate the claim and the neurology whereby you could conceive of it? This is the reason for the Rasul's (s.a.w.s.) claim that not even he will enter the garden other than by the mercy of Allah.

The fact of the matter is that when we act on the basis of what Allah wants from us now, there is a benefit to us now. We open up the garden of delight in the immediate present called unconditional motive. In this garden there are many fruits. One of the fruits is freedom. A man who wants nothing in the future is not manipulable. He has no hand holds. Yet another fruit is security. If what makes me secure is what I want from life I will very rarely be secure, because the universe rarely delivers a set of conditions that are entirely consistent with my expectations. However, if what makes me secure is the quality of my contribution to a situation I will always be secure because I always have control over how I respond to things.

The most precious of the fruits of unconditional motive is ecstasy. The man whose attention is not caught up in the illusion of a future has all of his attention available in the present. He then has the attention to see what is in the present and if he does that he will see that it is extraordinary, truly delightful and meaningful. He will see the countless wonders that most people miss because they were looking the other way, elsewhere, over there, in the future. You see, we stave off our lives, we stave of what is immediate for what is far away, and we stave off what is approximate and real for illusion, for wahm.

We do not see things as they are and the reason we do not see things as they are is that we are not available to them in the moment which we are in. The reason we are not available in the moment which we are in is that our imagination is stuck. It may be stuck somewhere in the past, fighting some dispute with some person that upset you; or more often than not, our imagination is stuck in the future. 'Oh, what am I going to do now', or 'what am I going to do to him' or 'how am I going to feed my family, what about my job' or, 'who, what and when?' We have all of this stuff in our heads, cluttering up our minds. So we do not see what is actually going on around us, we are blind in the moment.

How often have you not seen somebody walking through a gathering being completely discourteous, but quite unintention- ally? This happens because the person is distracted, they are busy in their own head, so they do not notice somebody greeting them, or the person they have brushed aside or stepped over. We all do this sort of thing from time to time. We are discourteous because we are not present, we are absent. We are absent because we are carrying on some illusion, some drama of our own.

There are a number of medicines for this, but all the medicines are essences of the same root, and that root is the proximity of death. Your sajdah is a practice for death, because it is a practice of collapsing, of giving in, and of handing over your own illusion. Your dhikr is a practice for death, because it is about shutting-up inside, and shutting-up means that you do not assume that there is something coming after the moment which you are in. You are present in the moment which you are in. It is only by the dhikr of Allah that the heart will become tranquil. It is only by seeing His traces around you, seeing His handiwork, that your heart will be satisfied. Why is that? It is because your heart has been made in order to be satisfied with Him alone. The only reason why we have been made is to worship Allah. To worship means that you are constantly amazed and surprised. Look at what He is like. Al Hamdulillah. Subhaanallah. Just look at that, isn't it amazing?

However, you can only have that response if you see the thing, and the thing that He is trying to show you will always be in the moment. It will never be outside of the moment, it will not be in your imagination. Every moment which you are in is therefore miraculous.

We seek to find evidence of Allah by looking at the unusual events. It does not strike us that the day to day existence is absolutely extraordinary. It is completely miraculous. Why is it that the atoms of your hand continue being together in such a way as to give shape to your hand? Why don't they just scatter? Why should you have a hand? I mean, your hand is breathtaking. And more than being an object, it is an object that is animated. It moves, and more amazingly, it moves by your will. How does this happen and how has it come to happen?

We are walking in a sea of inexplicable wonder, every single thing is most extraordinary, and is beyond our comprehension. If only we would reflect. If only we looked at the thing and saw it for what it is.

The challenge in this is our boredom, because our boredom makes us dismissive. 'Oh, this is just a hand, or, oh, that is a simple movement.' Consider all of the spontaneous events that have to take place just for you to be able to get up from the floor, all the events that have to be orchestrated together, all of the muscles which have to move. If you think about it on a molecular level, that every single muscle cell moves because there are chemical messages being sent, this is really extraordinary stuff. There is no way that a human being can design a machine which could do that.

You are surrounded by miracle upon miracle, Subhaanallah. And we do not see it because we are not available in the moment. We are not available in the moment because we assume that we will be alive tomorrow. So, we sacrifice the real for the illusory. We take the cup of nutrients and of sweetness and we throw it out and fill the cup with sand; then we are surprised if the sand does not slake our thirst. Allah has told us that it is only by the dhikr of Him, that our hearts will be tranquil, because that is why we have been made. The digestive system has been made to absorb water, not sand.

Your being has been made to worship Him, not itself. You have been made to find Him significant, not to find yourself significant. This also means that you have been made to find Him in charge, and not to put yourself in charge. You can only find Him in charge when you stop trying to be in charge, when you have given up, when you have submitted, when you become restricted to the moment. This means you are no longer concerned with outcomes because you know full well that if Allah is going to take you now, He will take you and that there is nothing which can stop that. On the other hand, if He was going to give you life for yet another two weeks, then there is nothing that can take that life away.

So it is with every blessing. If He had intended for you the slightest good, there is no evil that anybody can do that could take that good away from you. If He had intended for you the slightest touch of evil, discomfort or pain, then there is nothing that you or anybody else can do that could avert that from you.

All inner traditions share a common theme. There are a couple of broad brushstrokes that make them all very similar. The first common theme is; 'Be here, now.' Shut-up and stop trying to take charge.

Give up your internal dialogue and for a moment be available to what Allah is putting in front of you, because if you recognize what He is putting in front of you, you will be so astonished you would not even want the thing which you are trying to work out for yourself anyhow, because the thing which He is giving you, is actually better than what you could want for yourself. Closely associated with the instruction that all of the inner traditions have, of being here now, is a similar instruction, 'remember your death'. Make your death proximate, put it on your shoulder, make it your advisor, because it puts things into perspective, and the perspective which it puts things into is 'you just do your best and you leave the results to Allah. The results are not your concern.' So you are at peace, because you know that you have done your best. What else is there to do?

We know that we are taught: 'Look at what has come be- fore you and see if you can find any fault.' When you look at your life ask yourself if it was up to your own ingenuity, could you ever have worked out the path which has brought you to where you are now? The answer to this has to be no, unless you are unspeakably conceited.

It was always guidance which pulled you forward; it was never your own ingenuity. Left to yourself, you would still be wandering around in your nappies. Left to yourself, you would not have the imagination higher than that of a 3 year old, it is not possible. So, you did not make yourself, you have been made. The being which is in the moment right now is not your creation. It is the out- come of a stupendously orchestrated set of biological and social events that no human being could possibly have arranged. If you understand that, what becomes apparent is that your life itself and the most precious things about you life are the outcome of unsolicited and unconditionally bequeathed gifts which you did not and could not earn.

You cannot earn who you are, it is not possible. Surely if you understand that then the only thing left in your heart can be gratitude, and the understanding that Allah has taken care of you to where you are now. This gratitude changes the inner environment to an environment of fullness which is quite different from the emptiness of need. We are so used to thinking of all motives as being concerned with getting things, that we see it as an emptiness that seeks to be filled. However, the grateful heart is a fullness that spontaneously empties. It may look the same from the outside but the inner reality is quite different. In both cases there is motive, but the structure of the motive is entirely different.

If I can look at my past with deep gratitude then surely it must occur to me that if He took care of me in the past He would surely take care of me in the future. So do what is required of you in the situation that you are in so that you can relax and enjoy the show. If you see the show as it is, you cannot help but be amazed and enchanted with the genius of the playwright.

And you know, this is secretly what we all really want. The average person is just waiting to sit back in the armchair of Allah's Mercy. It is like a person sitting back in a chair, exhausted, tired of having to keep themselves erect all the time, thinking that they have to, when all that they really have to do is to sink back into the chair. Sink back into that Presence which is all-encompassing, which is the essence of your essence. Take council from that. Take succour from it. Know that you are going to die and that it could be right now.

I once had a conversation with Imam Gafielien, the late Imam of Bosmont regarding prisoners on death row. The Imam was an extraordinary man who among other things was one of the few Muslim clerics that was prepared to serve as chaplain on death row in the latter apartheid years. He did it for something like 10 years. He walked something like two hundred prisoners on their last walk, and counselled them as they stood on the trapdoor, and then he watched them die.

It makes for an extraordinary being to have that exposure to the raw edge of existence. He had counselled these men in their death row cells for weeks before their executions, and he said it did not matter how unrepentant and tough they were in that period, all that changed as they were being led to the gallows. He said; 'You know, up and till the moment that the men got taken out of their cells they might still be arrogant and protesting their innocence, but the moment in which they stood on the trapdoor they were as meek as lambs and they were asking for forgiveness of the people around. This was true for all of them. Not one of the two hundred was different.' If you knew that you were standing on that trapdoor you would not be so high and mighty, it is just not possible.

And, in fact, we are all standing on that trapdoor.

The Angel of Death, Malik al Mout's hand is on the lever and at any moment, any moment.... Give up this pretence of being in charge and you will see wonders.

There are a number of practices which are useful in taking your death as your advisor. The first is dhikr. The aim of dhikr is to silence the inner dialogue, and when this dialogue is silenced inwardly, you will see what is at hand. Understand also that it works 'vice-versa', when you become aware of what is actually going on in the moment; your inner dialogue goes away. Attend to what is real, and you will be quiet inside. The converse of that is; when you become right inside, you will see what is real. Attend to the real and you will become empty, you will be right inside. The one hand washes the other.

Another very useful practice is to do what we just did be- fore the start of the dhikr.29 Start off your dhikr with that. Pick at least 3 colours that you can identify in the room and notice all the things in the room that have those colours. Now close your eyes and find three different sounds that you can hear and rest you attention on them one after the other. Next pick 3 physical sensations which are actually happening to you and put your attention on them. You do that and you will be quiet inside and you will immediately have a more profound experience of the dhikr.

Understand also that after every waqt there may not be a waqt following. By waqt I mean every period of your life. Now, obviously as Muslims our lives are punctuated by prayer, so after every prayer just take a moment and think to yourself, it is quite feasible that I might not make my next prayer, therefore, what is actually significant for me now? A few moments of reflection on this matter is sufficient.

Whenever there are things which punctuate your life, any times when you stop and start, think: 'This may be my last time for doing this, therefore, what is really important in the next period? This can be done every day when you wake up, with regard to the day ahead. It could be at every birthday for the next year.

May Allah grant us freedom from our own fear.
May Allah make us aware of Him as our constant Companion.

May He make us companionable with Him.
May Allah grant us conversation with Him and comfort in Him.
May Allah grant us a gentle hand with the world around us.
May Allah grant us a just hand with the world around us.
May Allah grant us nearness to him.
May Allah grant us annihilation.
May Allah grant us death before we die.

Al Hamdulillah.

———

29: F.A. - i.e. to silence your inner dialogue by raising yourawareness of your surroundings and thereby deliberately take attention away from yourself,the past and the future.

Testing: Seeing the cracks enables you to deal with them
Discourse 13: 15th June, 2001

Bismillahir Rahmanir Rahim:

There are two assumptions one can construct one's life on and there are possible variations of themes. The first assumption is that there is no one in charge. That existence is a wild set of random accidents, that the world is a dangerous place and that you have got to spend your life being careful and watching out, and working very hard in case the sky falls on your head, or some equally awful fate befalls you.

The other assumption is that there is someone in charge, there is a Manager to this affair called existence. These two different worldviews create two different engagements with existence because they are like premises; they are basic assumptions about life around us in terms of which we construct our entire internal dialogue. The person who is fundamentally convinced that the world is a wild place that does not have a manager in charge has a very noisy inner realm, necessarily so because they have to work it out for themselves all the time. They have to plot the next step. They have to take on every single situation that confronts them from the point of view of getting an outcome from it that is to their best advantage. This best advantage is constructed on the basis of whatever it is that they are trying to get from the other or avoid from the other at the time.

On the other hand, a person who assumes that there is a Manager to the affair and who knows that Allah is in charge, is a person who probably comes across as being a little bit naïve. They are very quiet inside.

They do not have too many opinions about this or that. They are not concerned about what they need to do to maximize their advantage of a given situation. They are not trying to protect themselves, and as a result they do not have too much to say to themselves or to anybody else.

This indicates that being a believer is more than just pro- fessing some Arabic on the tongue, or prostrating five times a day for 'Salah'. Being a believer means that you stop trying to take charge of the affair, that you stop trying to work it all out.

To spend your life trying to work things out to your best advantage and to try to make sure you get what you want out of life is belying your faith. You cannot say on the one hand; 'La illaha illAllah', that there is nothing that is significant and worthy of worship other than Allah, and then spend your life pursuing things that are fundamentally worthless; things other than Allah.

You know that you cannot be a Muslim like a Christian is a Christian; it is not a part-time occupation. It is not a Sunday affair. It is a total transformation of your life. It means cultivating awareness of His Presence at every turn. Awareness of His Presence also means that one is aware of the fact that He has given to you whatever you have at that particular point in time. **30**

Whatever has befallen you can only have come from One Source. Whatever befalls you only befalls you for one reason, and that reason is for your good, because that is what He promises, even if the medicine is bitter it is for your good. There is no power other than the power of Allah. There is no plot, which can be plot- ted against you, other than by His leave. There are no jinn which can be sent to you other than by His leave. You are not vulnerable to anything other than what comes from Him. We know that the Rasul (s.a.w.s.) said that if Allah has decreed for you the slightest amount of good, nothing in the world will stop that from happening to you. And if He has decreed for you the slightest amount of harm, nothing in the world will stop that from taking place.

There is no Agency other than Allah. If you understand this, you become free, you see, because so much of our lives are caught up in trying to work out and respond to what we think the other is trying to do to us. This can go to the extremity. Perhaps a black cat crosses the road and you spit over your shoulder, five times, or something similar.

You make your life unbelievably complex with all of these things that you have got to do in order toward off the plots of others, and the evil of others, and you go mad. It is not possible. **31**

Take Him as your Protector and you will need no other, because He is the Source of harm. There is nothing that can be- fall you other than by His decree. So, stop looking at the agency, stop looking at the hand and know that there is an Actor behind the hand. Know that this is both in terms of the Blessings and the Curse. See the Giver behind the hand that gives, and the same Giver is behind the hand that does you injury. **32**

You are only vulnerable and can only be vulnerable to that which you need to learn. You can only be vulnerable on the ba- sis of your weaknesses. Your weaknesses are defined by your own conditionality. A person who has a lot of fear will develop an ulcer; they will have a weak stomach, so they will get a lot of pain in their stomach. This means that they have created this physical affliction themselves on the basis of their fears. They have made themselves vulnerable in a different way to a person who for instance drinks too much alcohol or smokes too much and so makes themselves vulnerable.

We can only be injured in the way in which we make ourselves vulnerable. Your vulnerability is defined by that which you want from the world. Every single element or item of need which you have of the other is the lack in you. That area is where the other has the power, and in that area you are vulnerable. Then if the vulnerability is there, that is where you are going to get the injury. You must have experienced this; you have stubbed your toe, and within two hours you hurt the same toe. Why that toe? It is because your being has been made vulnerable there.

So we cannot be hurt by the other, the other can only hurt us on the basis of our own vulnerabilities and we have got to take responsibility for our own vulnerabilities. In fact, the hurt which we get from the other is a blessing, because it is precisely that hurt that makes us attentive to our own vulnerabilities, attentive to our conditional motive. When we experience distasteful or unpleasant things in our lives we should understand that that unpleasantness has been brought to us by Him. It has not been brought by the person who was the bearer of the unpleasantness, but by the Hand behind the person who has caused the unpleasantness, by Allah. He has brought you that unpleasantness precisely so that you can discover where your weaknesses are. That is why these things happen to us.

I will tell you a story about this which I think really demonstrates the case. Five years ago I was sitting in the khalwa at Umdeni, and Sidi Alaoui was serving me. One night I heard a commotion outside the khalwa but I ignored it, because I was not permitted to come out. At the end of this process which I think was about three or four days later I came out and Sidi Alaoui related a story about being attacked by a jinn, and of hands coming out of the khalwa and slapping the food off the tray. I was utterly unaware of this, but then you see, I will always be unaware of these things because I do not take these things seriously. You cannot spook me because I do not believe in spooks.

You can only be vulnerable to that which you make yourself vulnerable to. The whole of life is like that. When you make yourself vulnerable to something, that thing will come and visit you. It will come and visit you so that you have to deal with it, so that you can examine the outlines of your weakness, of your conditional motive. This is why Allah brings us misery. It is to show us our own conditionality, our own cracks, our own weaknesses.**33**

So, the next time somebody causes you discomfort and pain, before you rush to stick a stiletto through their head, just ask of yourself, 'what is the blessing in this for me?' It is only once you approach an event from this point of view that you are appraising the event correctly. It is only once you recognize that whatever happens to you is for your own benefit that you can respond correctly in any given situation.

To believe means to profess, to understand and assert that Allah is in charge. He is 'Rahmanir Rahim'. He is the Benevolent; He is the Granter of all things. His charge is the charge of the Kind Master, the Master who seeks the best for the slave, and gives the slave that which the slave requires in order for the best in the slave to be realised. So whatever happens to you happens from that point of view. It only happens to you from that point of view. So, while you are not experiencing gratitude in your heart when things go wrong you are not seeing the thing as it is. You are somehow mistaken with regard to it. You are not seeing it correctly.

———

May Allah grant us freedom from our own fear.

May Allah make us aware of Him as our constant Companion.

May He make us companionable with Him.

May Allah grant us conversation with Him and comfort in Him.

May Allah grant us a gentle hand with the world around us.

May Allah grant us a just hand with the world around us.

May Allah grant us nearness to him.

May Allah grant us annihilation.

May Allah grant us death before we die.

Al Hamdulillah.

———

30: And that it is the best that you couldhave at that time.

31: A.A. - In the words of the famous Kristofferson/Joplin song, *"Freedom's just another wordfor nothing left to lose."*

32: A.A. - Be with the One Who Contracts, not with the contraction. Be with the One Who Expands, not with the expansion.

33: F.A. - Allah tests us so we may see what we are made of.

KNOW YOURSELF AND YOU WILL KNOW YOUR LORD
Discourse 14: 22nd June, 2001

Bismillahir Rahmanir Rahim:

We know from the deen that the inverse or the opposite of belief is kufr. We also know that kufr means or is derived from the Arabic word that means to cover or to hide the Truth. It is to cast into darkness that which is correct, or that which is real. In other words, it is about dishonesty. It is about lying.

It is interesting that this lying has within it this element of darkening or hiding. If you have a look at how people function; very few people deliberately set out to fail at the project of their lives. Even the most perverse and disturbed people who are acting in a way which is destructive are doing this because on some level they have convinced themselves that this will bring them happi- ness. That is why they behave in that disturbed way. If there were not a conviction somewhere in their hearts that their actions would somehow bring them happiness, they would not behave like that. So, there is within us this capacity to delude ourselves.

A kafir is not just a person who is hiding the truth from others; more significantly, he or she is a person who is hiding the truth from him or herself. They are covering the truth from themselves. This is the most extraordinary capacity which people have. It is to fool themselves. Now, this fooling of our self has a very complex coding, which is not that easy to decipher. We all hide things about ourselves from ourselves because we cannot bear to look at them. We are all in that sense kafir.

There are very few people, save the absolutely enlightened, that do not suffer from this self-delusion.

This is one of the significances of this statement; 'Know yourself and you will know your Lord.' One of the interpretations that Shaykh Fadhlallah has put to this is that knowing yourself means be honest with yourself. Be real with yourself about your own pettiness, limitations and vices. If you do this you will recognize the beneficence, the generosity and the mercy which you float around in.

So we all have elements of kufr within us. We all have elements of hiding the truth from ourselves within us. We all have elements of chasing the shadow, of chasing the illusion, of pursuing that which we think will bring us happiness. Decoding these things is a little bit like trying to see the eyeball which you see by. These things are so close to ourselves that we cannot see them, because they are ourselves.

From one point of view the nafs is nothing other than a web of illusion. It is a web of pre-conceptions that have basically been formed historically. They come from the past. The only reason why you believe that you are a man or a male is because you have had countless affirmations to that effect from the world around you. Now you walk around with a linguistic program in your head that says that you are a man. We know that the ruh is singular which means it is androgynous. This means that at the deepest, subtlest level even your gender is a lie. It is not who you really are.

Anything, which you can say or assert about yourself is at the same time, true and false. The degree to which it is false is the degree to which it is part of the illusion which keeps you trapped in the cage of who you think you are. For example, you are walking through a crowd and somebody calls your name, and you look up. That programming is kufr in its subtlest sense. That idea that that noise refers to this looker who is walking through this market is an absolute presumption. It is a historical accident. The name does not equal the one who is looking. The conviction that the one who is looking has that name and that that name refers to the looker is false.

You cannot know who you are without dying. You cannot know the limitlessness that is at the base of your being without giving up the limitedness of your assumption of who you are. The limitedness of the assumption of who you are is a series of veils, a series of coverings - of kufr.

This suggests that our common usage of the ideas of 'kafir' and 'muslim' is a very clumsy legacy. When we assert 'I am mus lim and he is kafir' we hide the most obvious truth of all, and that is that we have far more in common with this kafir than we would like to believe.

A person on the path is humble. So what does humbleness mean? It means that you are not presumptuous. We do not carry falsehoods about our own significance. We recognize that all we are is a moment of looking, a moment of consciousness. Conscious- ness has not been designed to find itself fascinating. Your eyes have not been made to find you fascinating. They have not been made to look into the back of your head. That would look extremely ugly. Your eyes are symbols of consciousness. They have been designed to look at the other. This means that your consciousness has been designed to find the other fascinating. We are here to find the other significant, not the self. This is the core rule behind all courtesy. Courtesy is you saying to the other 'you are significant, I treat you with respect. I treat you as significant. I do not claim significance, I grant the significance to you.'

In any instance where you claim significance, you are lying to yourself about your own nature. Your nature is not the one who owns significance. Your nature is the one who grants significance. The looker is not looked at. Assuming that the one who is looking through this thing called your identity is your identity is a false assumption. You can separate everything about yourself from that within you which does the observing.

It is like most of us who have had the good fortune of coming into the deen from outside of the deen. You know that you can change something as apparently definite as your name at the drop of a hat; you are called something else, just like that. So, you are now no longer 'Fred', you are 'Fareed.' Amazing. The thing which you regard as most intimately connected to you is your name. If you choose you can change it like a glove, like a jacket. It is not the looker, the subject. It is an object, a very interchangeable object. Similarly, you say, yes I am here, I am this body, but you can look at your hand, in other words, your hand is also an object to you. You can see it. The looker is not that which is looked at.

So who is the looker? You are not your name, you are not your body, and you are not your thoughts. What is this? This point of observing which sits behind your being? That which shines through your being that which gives the world attention, what is this? This looker is not who you think you are. You think it is you, or who you think you are, be it Fred or Fareed, who is doing the observing and the appreciating of the world around you. Your assumption that it is your identity which does the looking; is both kufr and shirk. It is granting significance to that which should not be granted significance.

La illaha illAllah. There is none other than He which is significant. There is none which is worthy of worship, of being the object of awe, the object of undivided attention other than Allah. We know that Allah is outwardly manifest. Wherever you turn is the face of Allah.34 You cannot escape Him. He is immediately in front of you. He is immediate. He is apparent. He is the Object. Attention has been made for Him.

But what is this attention? The seer, we have just demonstrated, is not your identity; it is that which looks through your identity. It is hidden, disguised as your identity. Allah is inwardly hidden. So your being is a platform from which He can view Himself. The tragedy of the human condition is that the platform has become conscious of itself and has made itself the point.

If you went to a lookout point that looks over a vast and majestic view and over time it had been built up so much that the view had become obscured you would be disappointed. And so it is with us. We are disappointed with our life because we are looking at ourselves, not at The View. What obscures our view are the walls of covering the truth, the most disabling covering being the assumption that we exist separately.

This suggests that one of the most important attributes that you need to make a success on the path is honesty. It is your honesty with yourself, your brutal honesty with yourself, which is the thinners which strips away these layers of paint that we stick over the reality of who we are. Part of this honesty is to be honest to yourself about your own arrogance. When you catch yourself out, say 'aha you see, you thought you were significant, now just look at what happened. You thought you were so holy and that you we are so humble and then somebody did not greet you and you got angry. Ah, is that not interesting?' Why did you get angry?

This does not occur to most of us. The first thing we do is to go and attack this fellow who did not greet us. In the meantime he has stubbed his toe, or he had just had an argument with his wife, or there is some other good reason for him not having greeted you. He actually requires a little bit of compassion, not judgement.

We are not honest with ourselves, with our own inner dialogue and with what is going on with ourselves. This also suggests that we cannot be honest with our selves, if we are not observ ing ourselves. We need to start functioning from a place which is deeper than our assumption of who we are. We must be able to observe our thoughts from a place that is not within our thoughts.35 Most of us think that we are the noise in our heads. We do not realize that we actually come from a much deeper place, much deeper than the noise in our minds. You can only start getting a handle on the noise in your head when you no longer confuse it with yourself. This happens when you start pulling back. This is one of the attributes of reflectiveness. Reflectiveness means that you function from a deeper place, a place where you are not those things which you assume that you are. You do not just assume that this hand is part of you. You recognize that you are not this hand. You recognize that you are not your emotions. How can you be your emotions if the one minute you are up and the next minute you are down? Does that mean that you stop existing as emotion 'X' and start existing on emotion 'Y'? It does not work like that. I have thoughts; I am not the thought.

This means that there can be a whole menagerie of creatures crawling through my being and I can watch them like creatures on a movie screen. They are not me. I see them. It is only with that element of reflectiveness and functioning from a deeper place that it becomes possible to be honest with yourself. So for example; I walk down the corridor and Sidi Qasim does not greet me, so I immediately lash out, shouting 'you awful, discourteous, terrible man'. I shout at him, like that. Before I even know what is going on, it has happened. In other words, I get completely overtaken from behind, by my own inner dialogue. I do not stand in the third place where I can see his discourtesy to me and my reaction to it on the same screen, so I can choose my reaction. I experience my anger as me, so I can only act consistently with it. If you do not stand at a third place, a separate place from your own inner dialogue, you cannot do anything other than to react on the basis of your own knee-jerk, your own immediate, flash response.

So, if you are serious about being on the path and this is the project of your life, you will engage in activities of reflection, meditation and dhikr.

It is precisely these activities which silence the inner dialogue. It is these activities which enable you to witness that you are not your thoughts.

You actually see your thoughts as part of a broad can- vas of objects and they do not overtake you or define how you respond. You recognize that this is how you are feeling, that this is what you are thinking, but you have a choice as to how you respond. We cannot choose what Allah puts in front of us; so if the issue of our lives is what happens to us we are in bondage. We can choose how we respond. If this is the major variable of our lives we are free.

May Allah grant us success on the path.
May He grant us nearness to Him.
May He grant us annihilation in Him.
Allah, grant peace and blessings on our Nabi (s.a.w.s).

Al Hamdulillah.

Yearning
Discourse 15: 29th June, 2001

Bismillahir Rahmanir Rahim:

We are taught that everything which happens to us that is good is from Allah and that everything which happens to us that is bad, is from ourselves. Al Hamdulillah. At first glance one may question how this is possible since we also know that Allah is the Source of all events. If Allah is the Source of all events, how is it that we are the authors of our own actions? To understand this, it is useful to examine how we understand existence, our existence as human beings.

We are in a state of exile, we have been cut off from our home and we yearn to return. All yearning is a subset of the great yearning for completion and finality. Every particular thing that you desire affirms a lack of something, a part that has been broken off. If you are a man, you desire a woman. If you are a woman, you desire a man. If you are thirsty, you desire water. If you are hungry, you desire food. We are all lacking. We are all in a state of dis-repair, needy, seeking repair and wholeness.

We assume that that which is going to make us whole is the particular thing which we are lacking in that instant, but what we forget is that there is a deeper language of alienation and of lacking which we do not address by drinking the water or by eating the food. There is this element of wanting final completion, of absolute fulfilment. There is a neediness which is at the root of our existence as individuals. This is a fundamental sense of disquiet, and of discontentment.

It is as if we are all looking for a piece which has gone missing, and all other needs we experience mask this need, this emptiness and incompletion. Unfortunately, when we satisfy these other needs we are still empty. It is like scratching your hand under a heavy glove. The scratching does not actually hit the spot, or alleviate the discomfort. Our essential brokenness is projected onto a myriad of small perceived needs in a drama that reduces us to chasing a phantom, like a cat pouncing on the light of a laser pointer being moved around a wall.

In truth we are all pursuing the final placing back of the essential element which has gone wrong, which has gone missing. The human being in the world is a being bereft and lost, searching distractedly from the one side to the other side. We are running from Safa to Marwa, always sensing something missing. Shaykh Fadhlallah once told us that in the pagan days, the hills of Safa and Marwa had a female deity on the one hill and a male deity on the other. The running between the two was a ritual enactment of our basic disfunction as people. The grass is greener on the other side. If it is not here, then it is there. And when I get to the other side that then becomes a here, and I am still unhappy, so maybe happiness is back there. That is the journey of the sons and daughters of Adam.**36**

We come from Allah into this world and we ultimately return back unto Allah. This world is a time of separateness, of being apart from Allah. This is also our state of fallen-ness, but it is not useful to think of this as a fundamental badness or sinfulness. That state of being separate is by His design; it is by His decree, because it is only by having granted us our separate existence that we can, as a separate being, desire to go home.

He made us. He said that He made the whole of creation because He loved to be known. He had put us into exile so that we could have the delight of homecoming. So this is not because of a fundamental wickedness that we are in exile, it is part of the story. The extraordinary nature of this exile is that it is essentially an illusion.

Shaykh Muhammad Ibn al Habib writes in one of the qasidas of his diwan *"I asked my heart about the nearness of my Lord, It said there is no doubt He is present. So I said: What is wrong with me that I do not see Him? And it said to me: He is manifest in you."* If Allah is absolutely apparent, the most Existent of all existence, how is it that we do not have an immediate, palpable and tangible experience of Him? The reason is that we are veiled from Him.

Our exile is not the same kind of exile as if we were banished to America. It is not as if we have been placed somewhere else, because He is here. He is immediate. He is closer to you than your jugular vein. Your sense of alienation and of separateness is by illusion; it is by veiling and shadowing. Your individual existence is a web of shadows which hides the Essential Light that all existence comes out of.

The shadow confuses your individual identity with that which looks through your eyes. Behind your being there is a spark of wakefulness which is the essence of your existence. This spark of awareness wears a jacket called your identity; it wears the robe of your body. It is neither your identity, nor your body. It is some- thing far deeper than that, yet we think that we exist on the basis of our identity and of our body. That confusion is the veiling. It is the darkness.

Everything, which comes from the veil, is more of the veil. Everything which can come from the shadow is more shadow. This implies that when you try and do the right thing, your intent to get it right is part of the poison. There is a sanctimonious side to thinking that you are getting it right and that you are with the party of those who get it right.

Your goodness with a very big 'G' is a part of you demonstrating to yourself and to others and even to Allah that you are somehow significant. This significance makes your individuality exist, important and of note, whereas it is actually an illusion. It is not important, it is not of note. La illaha illAllah. There is nothing which is significant other than Allah. We are not noteworthy. So, everything, which can come from us, our 'Nafs', has to be further veiling and confusion. No matter how correct or how sanctimonious it seems. All of the genuine benevolence that comes from us comes from something which is bigger than we are.

If you look back on your life, and you look at the marvellous things which have happened to you, you must surely see that your life is laden with blessings and gifts which you cannot account for. If you do not see all of the great things which have happened to you, and all of the major insights you have had and all of the contributions which you have made, have all come from an element which is outside of your ingenuity, then you are lying to yourself. If you think that you have worked it all out, then you do not understand how your life works.

Your life is the product of an infinity of spontaneous processes which carry on without requiring your intervention or management. If it was left up to you, you would mess it up, because it is by definition more complex than the human being can manage. It is the Divine intervention in every human being's life, in every single step of the way, which keeps us functioning and alive. There is a benevolence that comes unbidden from an unpredictable corner, which carries you like a magic carpet into the next moment of your life. If that did not happen, we would be destroyed.

Left to ourselves, we are hideously dangerous to both our- selves as well as to others. The good which comes from us, is not from ourselves. It is good which comes from a Source, which is deeper than we are. In that sense we are like prisms, we are like lenses refracting the Divine Light. So when you do something generous for someone, it is not you who are being generous, it is only you for that particular moment. As Shaykh Fadhlallah would say; 'You are borrowing that quality of generosity which Allah gives through you, He is Al Kareem, the Generous One.'

If you are magnanimous, do not claim that magnanimity because it is not yours. If you think that it is yours, then that magnanimity is no longer magnanimity; it has become your own claim to significance. It is shirk. It is ascribing a partner to Allah, because He is The Magnanimous. Everything, which is truly benevolent, everything that is of haqq, of deep truth, does not come from you; it comes from a Source much deeper than you are. This Source has just chosen the prism of your identity to refract through at that particular point in time.

So when you are granted the grace to be generous, you should be twice as thankful as the person who receives the gift of your generosity. You should be thankful that you should have been used in this way. Al Hamdulillah. We are all in the deepest and the most fundamental sense not worthy. We are creatures of shadow. Our individual existence only exists as shadow. If that shadowing effect was not there, there would not be a place for our individuality, it would melt away or it would blow up.

When the drop goes into the ocean, there is only water; there is no drop. That particle of water in the ocean, which considers itself to be a separate drop, is totally deluded. It is allowed that delusion for a while and it stays in that delusion when it considers its own nature (as water) as being somehow unique to itself, and not part of the ocean which it is in. The ocean is the Benevolent, it is the Beneficence of Allah.

We are like the drop, and all that is of the water does not come from us, it comes from that which is His nature. The drop cannot claim that. All that the drop has is an illusion of separate- ness from the water. So the drop has its distinction, its veiling, its lack of benevolence, that which is contrary to the continuity and to the oneness of the water.

Shaykh Fadhlallah frequently says; *'If you want to understand the Generosity of Allah then look at your meanness. If you want to understand the Magnificence of Allah then look at your smallness. If you want to understand the Majesty of Allah then look at your pettiness, and so up to infinity.'* So this statement of 'Know your 'nafs' and you know your Lord' is quite an insight.

Know your veiling and you will recognize the Light which transcends the veil. Know your smallness and you will recognize the Greatness. The Greatness can only be recognized on the basis of your smallness. Your smallness is a product of His Decree; it has been made by Him for Him, because it provides the viewing platform from where His Significance may be witnessed.

This suggests that one of the greatest dangers on the path is the view that you can do all the right things necessary to stake your individual claim to both Jannat and to unveiling. Make no mistake; all of these unveilings which happen to you happen only by His decree. It has nothing to do with what you do. If you do not think that then have a look at people around you and you will see that the greatest murderers, people of the most shocking back- grounds, may be people who are of enormous inner insight.

On the other hand you get people who spend their lives studying fiqh and doing all these deeds to earn thawab's and they have hearts the size of a pea. How do you account for that? You can only account for it on the basis that Allah is the Opener. You do not open.**37**

All that comes from you is closeness and constriction. In my own life I can honestly not account for the best things that have happened. They happened despite my own will. I set off on a course which with the benefit of hindsight could have resulted in destruction for me and those around me. However, by a peculiar set of events completely outside of my control I was delivered to a place of protection. My whole life has been like that. I do not think that I am unique in that because that is the story of all the people I know intimately.

We are busy ferreting away at projects which will eventually destroy us, and then we get saved in time, time and time again. It is like a child running around in a busy road not knowing or realizing that there is an adult hand guiding, stopping, protecting and pushing this way and that way. That is exactly as we are with Allah. From our own ingenuity it is all a mess. It all works by Him. This proves that you can rely on Allah. Has He not brought you to this point at which you are now? Has He not always protected you? Has He not always stopped you from destroying yourselves from all the bizarre projects and arrogances around which you have built your life?

Demonstrably you are sitting here at this point in time, on this date, in this funny little place, not by your own ingenuity. So will He not continue to do that? We are not here to get it right. We are not here to succeed at the project of our lives. We are not here to make it all work. He has designed us deliberately in such a way that we cannot make it work.

This is so that we can throw our hands up in submission and say; 'You take over, I am not in charge, I cannot be in charge, because whenever I put me in charge, I make a mess. So You take over, You do it.' The moment that you do that, as Shaykh Fadhlallah would say; 'you will be amazed, you will be amazed, you will be amazed.' You will see things, which will astonish you. You will see demonstrations of Allah's Existence, Generosity, Beneficence, Mercy, Majesty and Justice which will be beyond your comprehension. The delight of that witnessing is the filling of all emptiness, the satisfaction of all need. It is the reason why He made us.

May Allah protect us from our essential arrogance.
May Allah keep us steady on the path.
May Allah keep us vigilant.

May Allah keep us loyal to Him.

May Allah make us careful of our pettiness.

May Allah grant us success.

May Allah grant us nearness to Him and annihilation in Him.

May Allah grant us death before we die.

Oh Allah, grant Peace and Blessings on your Messenger, and on his family and his Companions.

Al Hamdulillah.

———

36: F.A. - As in the Sa'ay, part of the rites of the pilgrimage in Mecca - rushing from Safa to Marwa7 times

37: F.A. - It is not the individual.

OUR INTENTIONS
Discourse 19: 27th July, 2001

Bismillahir Rahmanir Rahim:

When one participates in the (dhikr) circle, one eventually, in fact very quickly, starts to be connected by and with the other people in the circle. You stop existing as an isolated individual. The people who on a routine basis do dhikr together become connected in the unseen. That connectedness in the unseen creates the possibility of great openings for everybody concerned, because you have the effect of focussing, and of concentration. It is as if, when people sit in a circle, they become a lens that focuses the Divine Light to an intensity that burns out our essential dinginess, which means that there are a couple of important courtesies that one has to bear in mind in the circle.

One of these courtesies is that once you have sat in the circle for three or four times, you owe it to yourself and you owe it to the other people in the circle to continue, consistently, in the circle. It is by commitment to the circle that you are making a commitment in the unseen. Also, you start to understand that your own actions do not just affect you; they affect everybody in the circle. That is why there is a greater requirement of tolerance among people who continually do dhikr together, because it is like a pressure cooker that really forces out the most shocking things in people.

People who regularly sit together sometimes get up to the most extraordinary misbehaviour. This is because of the pressure cooker effect. It is as if the job that society or other people, or a community usually has to do for people, which is to surface their intentions so that those intentions can be clarified, is intensified. It gets fast-tracked and intensified when you participate in the circle. The only reason we are alive is to discover that we are not in charge. It means the giving up of all conditional motives. Not being in charge means that you understand that you are fundamentally incapable of managing any outcome of events which are beneficial to you.

You cannot do anything to the world to make things work either for your own benefit or for the benefit of others. Everything that comes to you comes from Allah. You are not capable of engineering your own good fortune.**50**

In fact, the degree to which you try to engineer your own good fortune is the degree to which you fail at the project of your life. This is how it works. There are two ways in which one can try to engineer a good fortune. One way is to do it malevolently, where you are trying to pursue just your own personal and individual good; where you engage in a transaction to get as much out of the transaction as you can, with very little thought of how you should be serving the person with whom you are dealing. You deal with other people principally on the basis of what you can get out of those people.

There is also a way of manipulating events which is for benevolent intent, like trying to be rational and reasonable with each other and among the group. We try and broker all of the conflicts in the group so that we can have ongoing negotiated settlements between all of the people. All of these attempts that we have to engineer outcomes are fundamentally flawed. Allah assures us in the Qur'an, as Sidi Qasim has just recited, that you can spend all the wealth in the world and you will not re-unite hearts. Allah is the Only One Who unites hearts.

You can have the most amazingly thought-out strategy to achieve negotiated settlements between people and they will ultimately fail. If there is not a common benevolence, of people giving unconditionally to the party, where they are not just looking at their own interest, but rather giving to give away; they are still attempting to manage outcomes. The degree to which they are trying to manage outcomes is the degree to which there will be disharmony in the group.

Giving to give away is an unconditional motive. Unconditional motive is basically handing the affair over to Allah. It is the degree to which we hand the affair over to Allah that He fixes and He heals. It is the degree to which we claim the affair that Allah leaves us to mismanage and finally destroy the affair and ourselves.

So being in a circle is the opportunity for us to explore the issue of motives. It serves to surface our higher intentions. We are all on this journey of clarification of motive anyway. Life is structured in such a way as to force us to clarify our true motive. When we are born we are here to get everything unconditionally. That is the truest statement for an infant. At day one the infant is owed whatever it is still going to get in the most unconditional sense of the word.

When we die we lose everything unconditionally. This means that at the moment of our death, we give everything up. We cannot take anything with us. We give it all. So our lives are pinned between these two unconditional moments; the moment of being here to get and the moment of being here to give. The direction of maturation is from birth to death. This means that the process of becoming mature is the process of the clarification of motive from being here to get unconditionally, to being here to give unconditionally. That is the process of growth.

"Innamal 'amalu bin niyyati." (Hadith). Verily, actions are judged by their intentions. Your intention can be one of two. The one is the unconditional pursuit of self interest, the other, the unconditional handing over of the affair (in other words, giving it all away). Inbetween the two we have various shades of grey. The degree, to which there is darkness in the shade, is the degree to which our own dinginess clouds or conditions our motive. Our dinginess is that aspect of ourselves which seeks to clutch on, which seeks to hold onto that what we think we want; what we think will make us happy. So we pursue a pretty girl or we pursue money, or we pursue whatever it is that we think will make us happy.

The degree to which we set these conditions and the conditionality of our beings is the degree to which we do not achieve the highest of our own selves. Our own fulfilment lies in being able to lose everything unconditionally. This conditional motive is designed to cause you only misery. Shaykh Muhammad Ibn al Habib says in his diwan: 'In everything other than the dhikr of Allah is pain and grief.' It delivers you only to a place of disenchantment, whatever it is. For example, you married a pretty girl and within a week you discover that she has halitosis.

Or you score this amazing contract and then within a week you discover that this thing is so fundamentally flawed, that you are going to be spun into bankruptcy within a month.

Whatever we think it is that is going to make us happy, actually just entrenches our sense of desperation. Our conditional motive, which says that there is something which we can get that will make us happy, is bound to fail. Happiness is not about what you get. Happiness is about what you are willing to sacrifice, to give unconditionally. That is the same as handing the affair over to Allah. That is dhikr. Dhikr is not just a little bit of noise in your head, a little bit of nonsense on your tongue. Dhikr means; 'I know that YOU are in charge. Incontrovertibly in charge. So here it is. It is Your affair, it is not my affair.' That is dhikr. Dhikr means that inwardly you are able to suspend the management of the affair. The degree to which you are managing the affair is the degree to which you're being is fundamentally sullied, it is dingy.

The whole of our lives is a struggle to combat our own dinginess. The peculiar thing about how this process of cleansing, of polishing the heart, of clarifying and cleaning up our own dinginess works, is that every moment of opening comes from Allah, it does not come from you. Every moment of expansion and of change is because you have given up, and that is vitally important. Do not think that you will change your dinginess by yourself, you will not. This is the Wahabi sickness, you see, that you become so prim and proper, that butter will not melt in your mouth, but in the meantime you are a monster behind the white-washed facade.

Understand that you are dingy because you have been made like that. You are His creature; He has made you with your flaws. He has made you with your flaws so that you can admit your flaws, so that you can be covered by His openings, by His Light. Whatever good comes to you comes from Allah. Whatever bad comes to you, comes from yourself. This means that when there is good, when there is an opening, when there is elevation of being, then understand that you did not do it. Allah opened it.

The only thing that you can do is to admit to your failure, to admit to your own dinginess. Try your best not to act in terms of it, but do not disallow it, do not disclaim it. Do not say; 'Oh, it is not me.' If you say that, then you have become a shadow-creature. You know, where your left hand does not know what your right hand is doing, because your right hand is getting up to such mischief that your left hand does not want to know what it is doing.

One needs total honesty on this path. You need honesty towards yourself and kindness towards others. Always ascribing the best possible motive to others and always having a very beady eye out for your own motives, for your own intentions, and asking Allah to cover them. Whenever you do that, things change and you change.

The purpose of being in the circle and participating in the circle is so that everybody in the circle can go through the same process of pressure-cooking. You see people getting up to the most astonishing things, and when that happens, do not judge them.**51** Understand that this is part of the pressure which you need to clarify your own motive. The degree to which somebody else's misbehaviour upsets you is the degree to which your motive is conditional. If your being was unconditional it would not matter what the state of affairs was that they have thrown at you, you would not be moved, you would not be in a state of disquiet. The degree to which your motive is conditional is the degree to which you need very specific conditions to make you happy. The more unconditional you are, the more that what others do, does not matter.

The sign of a faqir is that whatever he experiences from the other does not matter. When he is in the shade, he does not wish to be in the sun. When he is in the sun, he does not wish to be in the shade. The condition that the other imposes on him does not matter to him. The misbehaviour of the people around you is for you to see whether they can catch you or not. It is for you to see whether you still get rancorous about this, whether this still upsets you or not, whether this still gets up in your face or not. The degree to which it does that is the degree to which your motive is conditional. Do not try and go and change their behaviour, change your motive. Ask Allah: 'Look, I thought I had balance and now am off balance again. Astaghfirrullah. I thought I was in charge and now look; I am not even in charge of myself. I give up.' This is humility. This is self-effacement. This will reveal the moment of magic.

It does not happen in a context where it is all easy and light, you see. It only happens in a context where you put yourself at the edge because you want the best to happen. So when you are in the circle, be committed to the circle and participate in the circle. Understand that all the people sitting in the circle are connected to you, so be kind to them. Being kind to the world is being kind to yourself.

There is this wonderful Buddhist principle, that all things are empty of their own natures. If you have a look at your body, it has iron in it; your blood has iron in it. Where did the iron come from? It came from other than you. Your body has energy in it, so how did that energy get into your body? It came from the sun, it was photosynthesized through a leaf, and metabolised by a chicken, which you in turn ate. So in your body there is the sun, there is the leaf and then there is the chicken. In fact, as you are, you are a reflection of the entire cosmos. By disapproving of existence, you are disapproving of yourself. So be kind with existence, be kind to the people around you; be kind with the circle.

May Allah grant us success on the path.
May Allah make us committed to our dhikr.
May Allah make us committed to the path.
May Allah make us committed to the best in ourselves.
May Allah grant us kindness to others.
May Allah grant us carefulness with ourselves.
May Allah grant those of us who are ill, healing.
May Allah protect our wives.
May Allah protect our children.
May Allah protect our husbands.
May Allah protect this circle.
May Allah grant us success on the Path.
May Allah grant us nearness to Him.
May Allah grant us annihilation in Him.
May Allah grant us death before we die.
Oh Allah, grant peace and blessing on our beloved Messenger, and on his family and on his companions.

Al Hamdulillah.

50: *T.S. - But you have to try or you won't be able to see this for yourself. Also, you won't be available for or able to deal with whatever Allah puts in* *front of you. You won't actually live your life. The reason the author says these thingsis so that one can let go of outcomes and act on what is appropriate in the present moment. Trust in Allah, His Beneficence, and the beneficence of the world he has put us in.*

*   **51**: *T.S. - Although you may need to act to stop their behaviour, or avoid them for a while, if their actions are harmful and especially if they are illegal. At the same time, you realize that you are not responsible for their behaviour and intentions (hopefully you aren't complicit!), only for your own. Do not get tangled in their drama. If you get entangled, look at your expectations. What are you expecting out of the situation from that person? This should help you disentangle yourself.*

Annihilation
Discourse 20: 20th October, 2000

Bismillahir Rahmanir Rahim:

'He died in 1901.' Now, if one thinks carefully about what we are saying, it is actually a rather bizarre statement. At some point he was there. And then he was not there. And after he was not there, in what sense can he be said to have existed at all? Only that which is now, exists. Then, is not now. So it is as if he was never there at all. And this is as it is. Our fundamental resting place is in disappearance. As if we never were. Our lives are pursued as the endeavour to stand out, to appear. And yet, our true home is in the place of standing in, of disappearing. It is a place of obscurity where we came from before we were born, and it is the same place of obscurity we are aimed at via the grave.

We sing from the diwan of Shaykh Muhammad Ibn al Habib: *"Oh, you who wish to be annihilated, say all the time, Allah, Allah"*. This suggests that our fundamental pursuit is not the same as other people. We are people who pursue annihilation and disappearance like other people pursue standing out and appearance. Why on earth do we want a smashing of it all? Why do we aspire to the dismembering of our form, the complete obliteration of ourselves? What is it in us that makes us so impatient with how we are that we should rather have it destroyed than to continue as we are? When we pray for annihilation, that is exactly what we are calling for.

When we pray for annihilation we are saying that we find our own appearance, our own standing out, intolerable. We find the thought of continuing in the petty and fear ridden existence of a small creature who is attempting to stand out against the weight of the universe intolerable. We cannot face it any more. We cannot imagine another hour of this agony.

What is the agony that we are suffering that makes us so desperate that we are willing to smash it all? What we are calling for is not just for death, but for something far more profound. Utter annihilation. What we find intolerable is the excruciating imprisonment of our day to day lives, of being trapped in a prison of our fears and of our hopes, and our anxieties and our concerns. We are desperate for a life other than the one that we have. Paradoxically we cling on to the continuation of the life that we have.

We find ourselves in this impossible situation, of either having to change what we are doing because we find our lives intolerable; or battling to keep our lives the same, because we find the thought of changing intolerable. Laced through our day to day activity is a battle. It is a struggle to make our lives sensible and manage our affairs. To pursue what we want. However, we have been around for long enough to realize that there is a terrible anti-climax built into what we want.

So you desperately want to marry this woman, and you make this picture in your mind of the ideal life once you have married her, and so you marry her, and she turns out to be the biggest witch on earth. You work your guts out to score some business, and it so happens that you get the piece of work or business and this business is just trouble upon trouble. You know the caution: 'be careful what you pray for, you may just get it.'

The most dangerous things to get are those things that we think offer us a final solution to all our troubles. We become like people playing the Lotto. We fling a final desperate measure at life in the hope that we can somehow get to a place of arrival, where we will not have to do anything anymore and everything will be okay. A suicide bomber is doing this. He is throwing a last desperate measure at life so that he can get to the garden. As if he has any negotiating position with Allah.

Our day to day struggles are about achieving some state or outcome which we feel is better than what we have. Better is specifically about security and contentment. We think; 'when I have that then I can relax. Then I am secure.' Whatever we do, we do conditionally, in order to achieve a more fulfilled state, a more secure state. However, these things that we achieve are always anticlimaxes, and if you are in a circle like this, you have hopefully started to realize this.

You may remember your last year at school, your matric examinations. Twelve years of schooling aimed at this event that is going to deliver you to a fundamentally different place afterwards. You will be of the arrived. You will be one of the significant ones who have got the license to have a life. Your last year at school focuses on that last December as if it is somehow going to completely change you. However, you do these examinations and life just carries on afterwards.

It is as if life did not notice that you have written examinations. The same anxious person wakes up the day after the examinations as the one that woke up the day before the examinations. You went to the promised land of those with a university exemption but the little insecure and needy person that you were before comes with you. So the New Jerusalem of life beyond matric is actually the same territory. In the fullness of time, all the things that we struggle to achieve are in fact anticlimaxes, and one suddenly gets to the point of saying, 'but why on earth do I struggle, what is this all about? No matter how hard I strive to be truly remarkable, to truly stand out, inside I remain mediocre.'

This can carry on for decades. I go from the one anticlimax to another, from one hollow dream to another. I put up this thing as significant and I achieve this thing or it gets dashed, then I put up something else and you then come across a group of people who sing: 'You who wish to be annihilated say all the time Allah, Allah', and you recognize that the desperation and this unquenchable thirst cannot be quenched by anything that you yourself can manage.

You are in fact dealing with a problem that is too complex to solve, that is meant to drive you to the point of such distraction that you literally, in desperation, throw everything overboard. Ruthlessly, throw any desire for significance overboard and throw away any pretence that you have any meaning in this world. You jettison spouses, bosses, family, subordinates, children, and the whole charade because you have seen through the trap.

You see at the root of our desperation is a suspicion that we are trying to construct significance on something that is fundamentally insignificant. We struggle in order to be heard, we struggle in order to be seen, we struggle in order to be affirmed, to be made significant, and the struggle is fundamentally futile.

There is no point where you can say that 'now I have arrived, now I will be acknowledged until the last day', because everything vanishes, except the Face of Allah. It does not matter how important you think that you are, it does not matter how big and famous the history book is wherein your name is recorded. Within a hundred years you will not be particularly important. Think of all the millions of people who have lived, the millions of people who must have been alive a thousand years ago. How many of those personalities do we still have with us today, in text or in memory? Tragically very few. A drop in the ocean.

Extraordinary personalities, incredible people and they are all gone as thoroughly as if they never were. We may know of them as a group. We know the date that the Vikings came, but can we name the name of a particular Viking? These people conquered Europe. Now, a thousand years later, they are gone. When you stack the lineage of people next to each other rather than on top of each other there are very few people. Three lives span 200 years. Between a grandparent, a parent and a child we span 200 years. That means there are 15 people that separate us from those great souls who had Europe under their heel. That is not a lot.

Those brave men that went into the North Sea with their naked arms, and the freezing cold, and in those open boats, with battle-axes, fighting through the whole of Europe, are 15 people away from us. A small meeting away from you, and yet, as individuals, they are not remembered. As individuals they are not known, they have disappeared. They did all that battling to carve for themselves a niche in history but they have been forgotten.

Our desire to establish significance for ourselves is fundamentally flawed. It is not attainable. The blessing is that when you come to this insight it is at first utterly depressing, and then suddenly completely thrilling. The reason for this is that you are not here to be significant. You are not here to be affirmed, you are here to affirm. You are not here to be made important, you are here to grant importance, you are not here to be made significant, you are here to grant significance. You have not been made to be seen, you have been made to see. You are not here to stand out, you are here to stand in, to remove yourself far enough from the arena so that you can witness The One who is the only Noteworthy, the One who is Outwardly Manifest, Allah.

What you are here to grant significance to, is Allah. You exist to confirm and bear witness that He is the Plotter behind all plots. He is the Planner behind all plans. Whatever your ingenious plans are to make yourself significant, they will all be dashed. He will dash your attempt to make yourself a remarkable being against the wall of time because the pursuit of your own significance is a misapplication of your being. It has been designed for Him, not for you. He will outwit you and obliterate your illusions to demonstrate that He is the Significant One. Throughout history He has affirmed that those who put their heads low, who disavowed significance, were raised up, while those who made themselves important were destroyed.

So wishing for annihilation means; 'I wish to disavow any pretence of being significant, of being of any use, of being of any importance. My only role here is to bear witness to Him and that is why He made me. If I act consistently with that charge, my reward is with Him. Any other endeavour is futile, is doomed to failure and can only deliver me to a point of futility, despair and suffering. La illaha illAllah. There is nothing else to be pursued here, nothing to be granted importance other than Allah. All other things are a waste of breath and time. Everything else is silly and futile.'

We have to be led to this insight, and what leads us to this insight is failure. This circle is for those who have experienced this failure. Those who sit in the circle are peaceful, undistracted and undisturbed because they have pursued and failed frequently enough to have given up. Their eloquence is in submitting, not in commanding. It is handing over control rather than being in charge. They are undistracted and undisturbed because they cannot make their lives work. They are not like other people. They are not successful. Their eloquence is in loss and failure and not success and gain.

They know that fundamentally, the world of men, the world of family and of business and of work and of success is an illusion. They see all the good that they get from this world as blessing, not the result of their ingenuity. They cannot be seduced into somehow thinking that they can make a success of life.

It is His way that He presents things to us by way of their opposites. All the shaykh's teach us when we are in times of difficulty, when the world is hostile to us, that these are our best times.

When we have outer constraint, we have inner expansion. The times of ease when the world is kind to us are the most dangerous times. It is then that we most easily claim our good fortune to be based on own genius. With outer expansion comes inner constraint. That inner constraint is to suffer the affliction of arrogance and ingratitude. It is forgetting who you are, because if you know yourself you will know your Lord. You will know His significance by your insignificance.

May Allah grant us success on the path.
May He grant us nearness to Him.
May He grant us annihilation in Him.
Allah, grant peace and blessings on our Nabi (s.a.w.s).

Al Hamdulillah.

ALLAH IS THE LIGHT
Discourse 21: 3rd August, 2001

Bismillahir Rahmanir Rahim:

"Allahu nuru samawati wal ardh": Allah is the Light of the heavens and of the earth.**52** This is a comment on the nature of existence. This statement is true, not just on the basis of material fact, but it is true on an untold multitude of levels. Like so many things from Qur'an the significance is to be found in layer upon layer of interpretation, anything from that which is physically demonstrable to that which is purely metaphoric and allegorical.

Let us first reflect on nur (light). We know that before existence got condensed and reduced and cooled down to assuming material form, existence was light. This is physically true. That energy precedes matter and not only does it precede matter, but it is in fact, all matter. Matter is energy in a cold storage. It has less heat, is quieter, less agitated, stiller. All existence is originally light.

We have all come from a realm of Light. We are destined to return to a realm of Light. This brief holiday that we have in this place of density and matter is only a dream. What exists is light and that light is the garb, (the clothing) of Allah. It is Allah's manifestation. It is Allah's outward expression.

If we look at material existence we are confronted by a myriad of clamouring things. The combination of the elements is expressed in so many untold complex ways that we have all of this separation and distinction in the world of matter. The subtler you go, the more you deal with the realm of light, and the less distinctions there are. The more things relate to a single root of pure white light. To that which is the first emanation of Allah.

Material existence is light mixed with darkness. It is light in cold storage; it is 'chilled' light. It is chilled energy, so that the energy becomes increasingly quiet and cool. That is what creates the conditions for things to literally coalesce, like a clot, out of energy and into material objects, which we can see. So things come from Light mixed with darkness, mixed with coldness, with non-existence, and then become tangible objects. This means that tangible objects are light and darkness mixed. It is coolness, it is emptiness, and it is darkness mixed with light.

When things manifest, they first come from the realm of Light. A very good way to think about this is that the light, which is the pure white light of Allah, gets split, like through a prism. The one white light splits up into all the different colours of the rainbow. The One becomes the many. From the one Divine Name come all the Divine Names and Attributes. From the One Light comes all other light.

From Allah comes the Loving, through to the Judge. From the Life-giver to the Life-taker. From before the beginning, after the end. From that which is hidden to that which is manifest. All of the Divine Attributes come from a single Source. The Light of Allah goes through this prism of the first manifestations, and splits into these various expressions of Light, but they are all still Light. Allah in His garb of Al-Wadood is no different from Allah in His garb, Al-Haqq. It is no different from His garb of Ar-Razzaq and it is no different of His garb of Ar-Rahman

In other words, it is one single unifying reality that is reflected to manifest differently. Another way of understanding this is as if you are looking at a diamond with facets and each facet has a nature of its own. It has a reflection of its own, but yet it is still the diamond. So as things are created they come out of One Source and then you have the splitting into the Attributes. It is the Attributes that give animation and life to that which is dead. In other words, when light is mixed with darkness you get the light that creates a manifestation.

It is a Light of one of the Attributes. For instance, when Allah creates a mountain, the mountain is imbued with the attribute of Majesty, so that when we look at the mountain we are immediately in awe at the Majesty of Allah. When Allah creates a flower, He imbues the flower with the Light of

Beauty. So that when you look at the flower you are immediately reminded of the Beauty of Allah. This means that everything that you see, that which is visible, that which is apprehensible and understandable, is an expression of Allah. It is a refraction of Allah. Allahu nuru samawati wal ardh. Light is that which is. Insofar as something can be seen it is perceivable by the light of Allah. It exists by the light of Allah. It is a refraction of the light of Allah. If you do not see that, then you are not seeing the Truth.

Without that emanating, Life-giving, Essence which is from the One, which has been split through the Divine Attributes, there is no existence. For example, when you meet different people, their differences are based on different expressions of His nature. You see a very discerning person, or a very loving person, or a very generous person, and another person is a very courageous person. All of these things that they reflect are not the person themselves, but rather they are reflecting an attribute of Allah. Their beings are like vessels that carry that particular refraction of the Divine Light.

One may say that things also come from that person, and not only from Allah. However, what comes from the individual is only darkness. What comes from Allah is Light. Allah tells us that all good that comes to us, comes from Him, and that all darkness, all bad that comes to us, comes from ourselves. The self, the realm of physical existence and limitation is by definition the kingdom of darkness. This kingdom of darkness gets animated, when Light gets blown into it through the Divine Attributes.

When you see somebody behaving generously, you are actually seeing the Generosity of Allah. This is why the courtesy when somebody acts generously towards you, is to thank the slave and to thank the Lord. *"Shukran Allah, Al Hamdulillah."*

We do not have anything to give. We can only hope to reflect. This is why we Sufis pray to be coloured. Shaykh Ibn al Arabi used to talk about people taking on the colour of the attribute. This is why we would do 'Dhikr' on a particular Name. A person who does 'Dhikr' on 'Ya Kareem' often enough will become a generous person, because he will start being suffused by that Light. He is calling that Light from the Highest into his being so that he can radiate it. So that he can become a lens for it. Allahu nuru samawati wal ardh.

Nur is also associated with discrimination, of seeing things as they really. This means that all meaning works on the same principal as refracted

Light. If there was not One Source of meaning, all language would be meaningless. Language is a symbolic system of signifying, of pointing out. This means that all languages are based on the assumption that there is such a thing as the Significant. Allah is The Significant. It is from The Significant that signifying can come. This means again that when you truly understand something with your aql, (your intelligence), then what you are seeing is a Divine Manifestation. What you are seeing is a refraction of Allah.

You must have had the experience that when you are struggling with something that you do not understand and then suddenly you have an insight, that flash is Allah manifesting. In that moment you quite forget yourself, because you get so bewildered with excitement. 'I see, I see, I see.' This moment is temporarily being released into a higher realm of meaning, outside of the darkness and the ignorance of your limitations.

The kafir has the same experience, but because of their shirk, they cannot acknowledge the Source. Allah says He forgives anything except shirk. You can be the worst murderer and thief, but remain free from shirk, you are fundamentally safe. However, if you assign a partner to Him it does not matter how pious you are, then you are destroyed. Not committing shirk means that you are recognizing Allah in that which is around you, both in terms of the outer realm and in the inner realm. In the outer realm you see things as reflections of His Light. In the inner realm you recognise that all true insight is by His Light.

We all have the 'aha' experience where we were confused and in darkness, when suddenly we saw. That instant is the Light of Allah penetrating into the darkness of our confusion. It is His Light refracting through the specific lens of the problem that you were not managing to fathom. This means that Allah is truly incredibly close to us. He surrounds us all the time. Anything that makes sense makes sense by the Light of Allah.

You know, we speak about wanting Lights, we pray for openings, but we do not realize that making sense out of the simplest statement is an opening, it is a Light. Allah is not going to come to you with trumpets and chariots and golden horses. Allah is already there.

We want the extraordinary while we are in fact completely wrapped up, both inwardly and outwardly by the miraculous. How is it that a tree can become this majestic thing?

How is it that your hand can move? How is it that you can actually ingest the water? How does all of this work so spontaneously?

All of these patterns of things that exist are different refractions of the One Source of Light. So Allah is the Light of the Earth and of the Heavens. He is the Light of all that is seen and all that is unseen; of the outer realm, (the realm of manifestations), and of seeing and the inner realm of meaning.

May Allah keep us steadfast on the Path.
May Allah allow us to see Him in the smallest things.
May Allah allow us to catch a glimpse of Him in the smallest understandings and insights.
May Allah allow us to catch a glimpse of Him in everything that strikes us
outwardly, from the Majestic to the Beautiful, from the elevated to the base.
May Allah grant us success on the Path.
May Allah grant us annihilation in Him.
May Allah grant us death before we die.
Oh Allah bless our Beloved Messenger, his family and his companions.

Al Hamdulillah.

_____

52: The Qur'an: [24:35].

HUMILITY
Discourse 22: Undated

Bismillahir Rahmanir Rahim:

Shaykh Fadhlallah frequently quotes the narration of Shaykh Abdul Qadir al Jilani who described his passage to the Garden as follows: He said he went to the gate of worship and he found clamorous hordes of people there already. No way in. So he went to the gate of service and found the same thing, so many people. There was no way in, everybody was crowding around that gate. So he went to the gate of praiseworthy quality after praise- worthy quality, he went to gate after gate, and there was no way in. There were too many people there, too many souls clamouring for admittance. Finally he got to the gate of humility and there was nobody there. And so in he went.

This means that for us the gate of humility is the most accessible. It is the quickest route. It is the surest journey and the most guaranteed method of arriving, that is, if you want to arrive. Many of us say that we want to arrive; we say that we want to get out of the torturous anxiety of our day to day lives, the little patches of pleasure besieged by a sea of insecurity and discontentment. Yet we are so frightened to give it up that we are contented with the misery of creation rather than having the security of the Creator. The whole of tasawwuf, certainly the whole of the Shadhili tradition and within it, the whole of the Darqawi tradition is a study in humility. It is an understanding of how the soul progresses and how the journey of the self progresses by increasing loss and self-effacement.

Translated into a language that we are already familiar with, we know that if we want something from the world, the world has a hold on us. Shaykh Ali al Jamal referred to this hold as the chains and ropes of the world. If you want something from the other, the ability of the other to withhold what you want, makes you manipulable, it puts you under its thumb. You are under its control.

There are two things you can want from life. You can want things of the senses (form), or you can want things of meaning. In other words, you can either want material things, or you can want to be made significant, meaningful and important. The first thing, the desire for things, is dangerous to you; but it is not as dangerous to you as the second. If you want a material thing from someone that person's power over you only lasts as long as they have control over the object. Once you have the object in your hand their control over you ceases.

However, if you want that person's good opinion, or if you want that person to regard you as significant, you are in very deep trouble, because that person's good opinion of you never leaves them. You never actually gain control over that. This means that if you engage somebody else on the basis of wanting to be seen to be significant by them, you are lost and more manipulable. Now, gaining significance from an individual in a transaction is an instance of an even bigger disease, that of wanting to become significant, to appear to be the star of the show, to take centre stage, and of wanting to become important. And that is not saying that I want the person that I am dealing with to indicate that I am significant; I am saying that I want it all; I want the whole universe to indicate that I am significant.

Shaykh Ali Al Jamal explains that the demand for significance is the demand for Lordship. The station of Lordship is a station that Allah is immensely jealous of. Therefore your claim to be the significant one is the root of your undoing. He will crush you. He will bring that head held high in self-importance to the lowest place, so that you can understand your status. In other words, when you claim importance to yourself, what you earn from the world, the universe and from Allah, is negation and abasement: shattering.

Shaykh Ali Al Jamal says that the person who chooses for themselves significance and importance has abasement visited upon them by force. However, the person who chooses, of their own free will, abasement and insignificance has significance visited upon them by force. There is no one who becomes more honoured among people that a person who disavows importance. Watch this rule in action; by looking at people around you.

Observe the person who constantly moves aside when the accolades are being given, and never claims it, and always shows good courtesy, always thanks other people when they say nice things about him. That person, over a period of time, becomes really liked. That person becomes truly significant. The person who disavows significance is the person over whom the other has no hold. If I disavow what I want from somebody else, they no longer have a hold on me.

So the question is, what is the practice to become one of those who are humble and who grant significance rather than claim it. What do we need to do to occupy that high ground? The first thing is that we have to take our salah seriously and understand what we are doing when we are in salah. Salah is an exercise in self-effacement. A person's identity, their sense of uniqueness and individuality, is associated with their face more than anything else. A person in sajdah has no face, he has no identity, and he is no different than the person next to him, because both their bottoms look the same. In sajdah we all appear the same.

Going on Hajj shows us that we are all the same; sawm (fasting) shows us that we are the same; we are all equally irritable, hungry and short tempered. Zakat shows us that we are all the same, do not think that your money is going to protect you; you are no different from the other. There, but for the grace of Allah, go I. All of these practices are practices of the loss of significance.

This self-effacement has habits that one should cultivate. The first habit is the habit of reflectiveness and silence - not having an opinion. We are all so terribly opinionated. We have always got something to say. But when you look at your own opinion, very often you are struck by how presumptuous these opinions are. For example, here I am reading today's newspaper, and there is a fellow by the name of Hans Smith who is about to lose his job. I actually knew this man from the mining industry and before I can stop myself, I am five minutes into an inner debate about how awful he was, how much he has deserved his misfortune. All of these judgments carry a body burden. Disapproval is bad blood chemistry. So here I am feeling bad about someone who has in fact become quite irrelevant in my life. And, to top it all, he really was not that bad. He had a number of really redeeming qualities. For one, he was a very handsome man.

How on earth do I know if he is the same person that I met five years ago? I don't. Who knows? He might have lost a child; he might have had a deeply shaking catastrophe in his life that fundamentally changed him. In fact, he may have become a very different person by Allah's intervention.

We presume; we pass judgment all the time. We talk away to ourselves all the time. We always have an opinion. Don't have opinions. The more you disallow your opinions, the more you come to know; and when you speak, you speak with the absolute assurance of complete insight. No speculation, no opinions, but seeing, direct witnessing. The person who speaks from witnessing has very little to say, but when they speak; people shut-up and listen. This is because what they say falls like a bolt out of the blue. This person is something unique; this person has something to offer.

The first habit on the path is silence, withholding opinion. Shaykh Ali al Jamal says that in this world silence has precedence over speech. The reason for this is that silence is an attribute of slaveness and speech is an attribute of Lordship. Your station in this world is that of a slave. When you behave according to your station; you are confirmed. But when you negate your station by claiming to have something to say, you are negated. Now, test this; the next time that you meet someone who thinks that he has something to say. Say nothing at all, just look at him and see what hap- pens. Eventually he gives up, and who walks away as the idiot?

This is not about learning skills of manipulation. This is how things work. This thing of silence and speech is based on a very deep rule that the whole of existence is built on. The rule is this: in the realm of creatures the station of silence has pre-eminence over the station of speech. Have nothing to say. This is very strong medicine. It disconnects you immediately from the other person's hold over you. You are the one that now starts having the hold.

Understand that the one who is talking is the one who wants the attention. The one who is silent is giving the attention. So where is the real giving in this transaction? It is with the one who is silent. So the one who is silent is granting significance. The one who is speaking is the one who is claiming significance. And who has more power, the one who claims or the one who grants? Where does the real power sit, with the king or the king maker?

The second rule is disengagement in transactions. It means to be separate from the world, and therefore be gathered within. I have spoken about this before, but the people who have impressed me the most of all of those that I have come across over the last ten years have been the Tuareg because of their habit of veiling. It cultivates a completely different personality. Not only is it a statement of disclaiming significance and of self-effacement, it is also the downcast eye. The man who walks through the crowd, the aggressive crowd, with a downcast eye, is safe from that crowd. The man who walks through that crowd looking at this one and that one becomes their quarry. As soon as you look at them, you engage them. As soon as you engage them, you are in fact inviting a discourse, a discourse which is sure to leave you the victim because they are many and you are one.

The equivalent of having nothing to say is not looking for the attention. You look for attention by looking for the eyes, so don't look for the eyes. Look down. When you are walking through the crowds, look down. This has nothing to do with becoming weak and meek; these very simple rules are the roots of power. If you want to achieve the highest status of your life, then you will follow these rules.

All the practices of the deen are practices in humility. By that I do not mean self-assuming humility like; 'Oh, I am such a humble man, just look at how low my back is' It is the opposite. It is the disclaiming of significance. Another thing that Shaykh Ali Al Jamal said is that many arrogant people wear patched robes, and many humble people wear jewellery and fine clothing.

It is as if our lives are overcast by very thick clouds, and that these clouds are our inner-noise. On the other side of these clouds is a very brilliant sun. That sun is His nature. Every time you stop the noise, you make a gap in the thick clouds, and you see. You see what you would never have been able to see if the clouds (inner noise) hadn't gone away. Al Hamdulillah.

What you would see is that the whole story of existence is about worshipping. Worshipping doesn't mean jabbering away in a language you do not understand and doing strange movements with your body; worshipping means you are amazed at things that are going on around you. Every moment you are alive you are being snookered by Allah.

You are having a divine and beautiful prank played on you by the Great Prankster. As you walk you are walking through a theatre of miracles.

This is true in every moment of our lives but we do not see it. We do not see it because we think we are in charge. We think we are the significant ones with our hands on the reins. The only reason why He puts reins into our hands is for us to find out that they do not work. You think that you are pulling to make your life go into that direction, and then everything falls apart. You end up in the opposite direction. And then the opposite direction turns out to be better for you than the place you wanted to be in, in the first place. This is Allah's Divine prank at work. We have plans and He has plans and He is the best of planners. We are designed to have plans of our own, which are designed to be inadequate and to be brought to failure so that we can see just how magnificent His plans are.

I must tell you a story about this. In the smallest of ways we get shown the silliness of our plans. Yesterday I was in Durban at the end of a long trip, and as I was walking into the airport, coming back from Durban, I was looking for my parking ticket for the Johannesburg parking garage. It was gone. I had lost it. This was a big disaster. I was very upset by it; I would not be able to get my car out of the parking garage. How was I going to solve this problem? I plot and plan. So I eventually went and sat in the business class lounge, quite beside myself, because I did not have any way of getting myself home now, at that point I realized that I did not have any cash on me and this worried me immensely.

My internal dialogue ran something like: 'Now I did not have cash. Damn. I normally just pay with a credit card straight into the ticket machine, but can I do that at the parkade? And where is my credit card? Oh dear, not here. I only have my debit card in my wallet. And how am I going to do this now? There is not enough money in my current account. I know, I will phone my brother and get him to do an electronic transfer to my current account and hopefully they will take my debit card.'

So, I finally phoned my brother and started describing to him what had happened. As I was describing to him what had happened I noticed a man sitting opposite me making these weird gestures. Finally, since I was getting really irritated, I told my brother that I would call him back in a minute because there is a guy here who really wants my attention. It turns out that this man runs the company that manages the Johannesburg International

Airport's parkade. When we got to Johannesburg he took me to his offices and gave me a complimentary pass to get out of the parkade.

Now, you tell me that Allah does not have a sense of humour. Of all the people to sit opposite, I sit opposite the fellow who runs the company that manages the parkade. There I was trying to make my own little plan work, and the answer to my problem was sitting right in front of me, having to carry on like an idiot just to get my attention because I was so busy trying to work it all out. This is a metaphor for our lives. **53**

This does not suggest that we should do nothing. If I did not try to solve the problem, that man would not have noticed and my issue would not have been addressed. We have to commit to the issue and do our best and fail. If we do not commit we cannot fail. The point is the failure after you have done your best. It is only once you have failed and things have come right despite of you, that you can truly bear witness that Allah is in charge.**54** It is then that we can bear witness that we plan and He plans and He is the best of Planners. Allah teaches us through the tiniest of things and through the biggest of things. Wherever you turn, is the face of Allah. **55**

May Allah grant us conversation with Him and comfort in Him.
May Allah grant us a gentle hand with the world around us.
May Allah grant us a just hand with the world around us.
May Allah grant us nearness to Him.
May Allah grant us annihilation.
May Allah grant us death before we die.

Al Hamdulillah.

———

53: A.A. - A sense of humour is indispensable on the path. But often it is only in retrospect that we realize the humour ofan earlier experience or situation. A sense ofhumour, 'in the moment', is the greatest blessings.

54: A.A. - The point of failure is a time and place of inner expansion, because you have reached such an extreme of outer contraction. A sweet and intoxicating experience. The effort and subsequent failure are necessary. The so called mistakes have to be made.

55: F.A. - The Qur'an[2:115], also relevantis the verse *"For thus it is, all protective power belongs to Allah alone, the True one. He is the Best to reward, and the Best to determine what is to be."* [18:44].

WITNESS
Discourse 23: Undated

Bismillahir Rahmanir Rahim:

Allah is the mover of the wind. He is the rotator of the earth. He is the beater of your heart. He is the opener of the flower. He is the rush of blood through your veins. Allah is movement, eternal living movement. *"Qul Hu Allah Hu Ahad."* **56** He is the One, there is nothing that can exist outside of Him. There is no movement possible other than by His decree. There is only One Actor, and that Actor is Allah Subhanahu wa ta'ala. We are the puppets.

Allah is the root, the rest condition that all movement comes out of. So He is both movement and stillness. He is outside our capacity to comprehend. He is both sides of the extremity at the same time. He is before time and He is after time. He is the beginning and He is the end. Those things that present themselves as absolute opposites, He encapsulates in His nature, and so it is quite appropriate for us to consider that Allah is over and beyond our capacity to conceive or comprehend.

He is beyond our ideas of good and evil. He is self-subsistent. He is like the perpetual motion machine. He is a contradiction in terms; that which requires nothing to continue, yet by His leave all things continue.

Allah Subhanahu wa ta'ala has no dependency on us; He has no dependency on existence. Existence is His pastime, because He wishes to be known. He has created this theatre, He has written the scripts, He has put the breath into the lungs of every actor and given every actor the capacity to speak; and yet He is outside of the whole thing.

He is the commander of every movement, yet He is not contained within that movement. *"Lam yalid walam yulad."* He does not beget nor is He begotten. He is outside our understanding of the circle and the cycle of birth and death. He cannot be phrased to be understood as the father or as the son. He is the same thing at opposite ends of the scale, because we know that we come from Allah and that we go back to Allah.

"Innalillahi wa inna Ilayhi rajiun." We come from Allah and we return to Allah. The beginning and the end are the same place because they are Him. What is irreconcilable to us, what is represented as complete opposites to us, is simultaneously true for our Rabb. Allah is outside our capacity to conceive. Whatever we conceptualize of Him is both true and false. If we say that He is the Life Giver that is true, but if we say that He is the Destroyer and the Abnegator that is also true. If we say that He is the Vast and the Great that is true, yet is it not also true that an electron cannot circulate the nucleus of an atom without His leave? Allah is beyond the smallest and the greatest.

Our nature is to desire to witness Him, because He has made us like that. He has made us to worship Him. Worshipping means that you are amazed and enawed by the reality of something that you see or experience. Worshipping means being amazed. We cannot have that state through an intellectual understanding. We cannot witness Him on the basis of words. You can only witness His awesome nature by direct experience, because it is apparently contradictory.

Language does not allow you to consistently articulate and think of things that are simultaneously false and true, or apparently contradictory. You cannot sustain it. You cannot conceive of the inconceivable and stay sane. You cannot say that the biggest and the smallest are the same. This is madness. Yet, we can witness the inconceivable. However, in the pursuit of this witnessing we have to accept that no matter how eloquent they are, the words that we use to speak of Allah are very poor indicators of the reality that we are after.

The reality that we are after cannot be approached by being spoken about and cannot be gained by being studied in books. It is about state and it is about heart, and that state only happens when we have stopped trying to define His nature. Once you stop trying to understand it in your head is when you begin to witness.

I am saying that there are two ways of knowing. One is the kind of knowing where we fully understand the knowing by words; and as you get older you understand things better and better, and are far more accurate in your description of things because you have lived more. This knowing is a growing body of information in your head about what you know.

This is not the kind of knowing that we are talking about when we speak about the nature of Allah. This second kind of knowing you can probably accurately refer to as unknowing. It is witnessing with the eye that which is apparently impossible, or witnessing with the heart that which is not sustainable; that which is utterly bizarre. It is for the heart to see that the world as we know it is in fact appearance and that the reality is inconceivably stupendous.**57**

This witnessing is to turn everything you know upsidedown. It is to at once perceive Allah to be absolutely present and absolutely removed. To see Him in the same time in His Attributes of Majesty and His Attributes of Beauty. To see Him behind the death of the child dying of cancer and to see Him behind the birth of the fawn in the forest. The same Truth. The same wonderful, terrible reality outside of our description. All the practices that we are concerned with are practices that are deliberately about shut- ting down our assumptions. These practices create the conditions where we stop thinking so we can start witnessing. They help us to see with our hearts, not just to understand with our heads. They are all concerned with silencing our internal dialogue.

May Allah grant us success.
May Allah grant us nearness to Him.
May Allah grant us annihilation in Him.
May Allah grant us death before we die.

Al Hamdulillah.

———

56: The Qur'an: [112:1].
57: T.S. - Althoughat first glance,what is known may appear really mundaneand common sense.

Repentance and Courtesy
Discourse 24: 17th November, 2000

Bismillahir Rahmanir Rahim:

We know that one of the most pleasing things for Allah is the tauba or the repentance of somebody who has transgressed. This is not to be understood as a confirmation that we are all bad and so terribly guilty, but because He has made us with our infirmness. Allah has said that He has made us weak. This means that weakness and failure are part of our design. The issue to dwell on here is therefore not how bad we are, but rather to explore why the admission of fault and the sincere atonement of mistake and transgression are so pleasing to Allah.

It is because, in the moment of us admitting our mistake openly, we are the creatures that He made us to be. He made us inadequate in order to affirm His adequacy. He made us 'abd, the slave, to affirm that He is Ar-Rabb, that

He is Lord. He made us weak to affirm that He is all Strength. He made us lost, homeless, destitute, hungry, and thirsty in order to affirm that security, comfort, water and nourishment are from Him.

It is in our brokenness that we find the secret of what we are. In our inadequacy we can attest to His Capacity. In our own assumption of adequacy, self sufficiency and of being in charge we are at our weakest. This is when we are most dangerous to ourselves and to the people around us.

Allah has made us to worship Him. Worship means to recognize that He is truly beyond description, that He is everything that we are not. He is vast, He is all inspiring, and He is extraordinary. Now, all of that is only possible, all of that super-adequacy can only be affirmed on the basis of our inadequacy. The capability of the One who is Supremely capable can only really be attested to from the vantage point of the one who is incapable.

Shaykh Fadhlallah always says that the statement 'Know yourself and you will know your Lord' has its significance in the understanding of opposites. When you know your meanness, your pettiness and the selfishness of your 'nafs' you will by negation know the Magnanimity of your Lord. He is the opposite.

This is why the shaykh's warn us that our best times, when we think things are going well for us, are indeed our worst times. On the other hand, our worst times are in fact our best times, because it is once we are at a loss, once we have been knocked over and no longer know where to turn and are powerless that we are in a position to witness His Power.

We are at our best when we feel our selves in the hands of fate. It is at those times that we are the closest to being what we are required to be in this life. That is when we are the closest to surrender. The word 'Islam' means surrender, surrender means; no longer being in charge. It is symbolized by the takbir or the raising of the hands in takbir, which is the same gesture that a soldier surrendering in battle makes.

I give up. I am a prisoner, I am a slave, and I no longer have a mission of my own. I have tried and I have failed. I have tried to be in charge, I have tried to cover all the possible bases, and I have found that every time I close a hole, another hole opens elsewhere. Every time I fix a matter, another matter falls apart. When I look behind me, the thing in front of me goes to pieces, when I look up, the things below me go to pieces. I cannot fix it; there is not enough of me. The life that I have and the world that I live in is too complex to take charge of. This is what surrender means.

This is not depressing or self-destructive. It is in fact the point at which things come right, the moment when you say; 'I cannot manage this affair, You take it', He manages it miraculously, because it is His nature to make irreconcilable things become simultaneously true. He can make the fire a place of coolness, as He did for Sayyidina Ibrahim (AS). He can make the birds vanquish the elephants, as He alludes to in Surah Al Fil. He will make the small band overcome the big host, as He did at Badr. And He manages it with an eloquence that is truly breathtaking. We know that if you try to manage the affair, He will let you manage your affair and you will mess it up. Leave it to Him and He will deal with it most adequately, in the most beautiful, awe inspiring and extraordinary way. In a manner which is infinitely better than you can manage it yourself.

The secret is therefore to understand how to give in and give up; how to surrender. We know from the Deen that the internal expression of giving in; (in other words, I cannot handle this, I am not in charge); has an outer expression in terms of a code of behaviour - a code of courtesy. Courtesy means that you have stopped manipulating. It means that in every situation that confronts you, you are not looking at it on the basis of how you can manipulate the situation to get what you want out of it. You are now looking at the situation and asking yourself what Allah would want you to do here. You ask 'what is the most appropriate thing to do here? What is the most helpful thing I can do? What does Allah expect of me in this situation?' Submitting yourself to this requirement of the moment is what we understand courtesy to be. A courteous person is appropriate; they act on the basis of the requirement of the moment. A discourteous person is the oaf who acts as he likes,whether it is appropriate to the situation or not. The Rasul (s.a.w.s.) said that he only came to perfect good character. This means that he came to teach us how to behave.

He came to teach us courtesy. The whole of the path is about courtesy. Every situation that presents itself to you has a requirement from you. It has a price that you need to pay. It stipulates a gift that it requires you to give. That gift is the thing that you need to put in; it is the courteous thing to do in that moment. When you act on the basis of doing that courtesy, Allah will look after the rest. The rest is His problem. Do not make His problem your problem. The rest is His issue. It is not your concern. Do what He requires of you and leave the rest to Him. What does He require of you? He requires of you to act on the basis of the example which He has sent to us, the example of the Rasul (s.a.w.s). It is our be loved Nabi Muhammad's (s.a.w.s.) Sunnah that indicates to us the right thing to do in any given situation.

Shaykh Abdul Qadir used to say that the key significance between the haraam and the halaalis, that the haraam is that which,when you act on it, diminishes you, it makes you less of a being. The halaal is that which, when you act on it, elevates you, it makes you more of a being.

One can therefore also understand the halaal to be the right thingto do in a given situation, the correct thing to do.

What does Allah expect of you in the situation? Every time that you act on the basis of what He expects, there is a piece of magic that happens. You change and the world around you changes. It is as if every moment is like a little examination that you sit for. Now, let us imagine that you come into a country and you go into the Court of the King, and the King says; 'I want to give you a little examination' but you have no idea why he wants to give you this examination, or what the consequences will be. He then sits you down in a corner and he asks you to do the examination which you do and you pass the examination. All of a sudden the King makes you the First Minister of the Kingdom (the Khalif), he gives you more wealth than you have ever imagined, and he gives you the best house in the city, and so on and so on. It is like that. Every moment that faces us is like a little examination. If we pass that examination, Allah has in store for us better than what we ever could have in store for ourselves.

By design you are more than you think you are. What allows that design to come out is that you act unconditionally in the moment, on the basis of what is the right thing to do, on the basis of what Allah requires of you. If you do that, you do not have to worry about what comes towards you; it really does look after itself.

May Allah grant us success on the path.
May He grant us nearness to Him.
May He grant us annihilation in Him.
Allah, grant peace and blessings on our Nabi (s.a.w.s.).

Al Hamdulillah

Reprogramming Ourselves: Ramadan
Discourse 29: Undated

Bismillahir Rahmanir Rahim:

We are about to engage in the high point of the Muslim's inner life which is the month of Ramadan. In this month we naturally tend to pursue the higher and withdraw from the lower. Allah tells us that there are two principal reasons for us to fast. One is that we can learn compassion for those who are hungry and the second is that we can learn patience.

We have two faculties as a human being. We have a faculty for doing, for pursuing our own goal, for focussing our attention on that which we want and then we have another faculty for allowing things to be done to us. The second faculty is patience. It is being able to allow the world to pinch you without you reacting.

On Hajj you are told that you do not swat a fly. You completely distance yourself from the assumption that you can be of any use to yourself. You do not squash the ant that crawls over your foot, you behave like a corpse. You are in ihram. You are in your coffin. All of the practices of the 5 pillars are experiments or exercises to exercise this faculty of giving up, of not being in charge, of total submission. The salah is a way of giving up, of not pursuing your goals. So is the fast.

The fast is about withholding food, of stopping our habit of eating. We spend so much time of our lives pursuing goal directed behaviour, of acting to satisfy our desires that we have to be brought to a halt by external factors. We have to learn to stop. That is the great blessing of the fast.

The great blessing of the fast is an exercise in stopping. An exercise in allowing the world to be done to us, rather than us doing to the world.

Our attention can function in one of two ways. It can either function like a lion, like a predator where you are focussing on what you want to get and this is very much associated with one's eyes. All predators have their eyes placed in the front of their heads, like lions. This is so that they can focus and direct their attention to the goal that they want, to pursue it and to grab it. This is a predatory capacity. Goal directed behaviour is to hunt down the thing that you want. The problem with hunting down what you want is that you forget that in the process of hunting that you are sentencing yourself to a lack of fulfilment.

I am not happy because I do not have the thing that I want and therefore I pursue the thing that I want. So based on the conditionality of my being and because I am conditional, because I suffer lack, I have to act in the world like a lion out for the grab, out to get that which I want.

Allah tells us that the entire universe cannot contain Him, but that the heart of a mu'min contains Him. This means that within you, in your core, there is a capacity to have paradise right now; to have it all. Anything that you consider to be wanting or any lack that you have is already fulfilled, it is already there.

This need we have to pursue, that which we want, is really based on an illusion. Sometimes we have to pursue that which we want in order to get it, in order to discover that it is an anti-climax.**59** When we are going after what we want we get so distracted that we do not see what Allah is bringing to us and that it is better for us than what we want for ourselves. We are so concerned with filling our sense of lack that we do not see that our lives are full.

We have to start practicing another way of being in the world, which is the way of assuming that life is plentiful and not lacking. In order to be like that we have to develop a different way of experiencing. It is a way of withholding oneself, of not being predatory, but a way of sitting still. It is to allow life to come to you. It is the way of seeing of the deer, the deer has got is eyes on the side of its head so that it can pick up any movement that comes to- ward it from any angle. So it is designed to perceive what the world is bringing to it.

Allah has two main energies or forces whereby He constructs the universe. The one is Beauty and the other is Majesty. Majesty is that which imposes and which penetrates. Beauty is imposed upon and penetrated. If we see that we are fundamentally here as creatures and not as creators, then we have to accept that the core of our reality is a reality of beauty and not of majesty. I am not the master, I am the slave.

If we see that we are fundamentally here as creatures and not as creators then we stop trying to govern and we allow ourselves to be governed. One of the key ways in which we govern is around food and eating. If you stop eating you are telling your animal self that you are not just here to consume, and to be patient because it will be fed, but not right now. So you are allowing the world to impinge on you. You are not going out to satisfy your hunger.

So all of the pillars, the sawm, the salah, the zakat and the hajj are all practices concerned with giving up. It is their principle aim. This practice allows another faculty to develop, another way of experiencing life. A way of experiencing life where we do not take charge but where we allow ourselves to be taken charge of.

"Verily actions are judged by their intentions." Based on your intention you have the reward of the action. It does not help when you start the fast tomorrow to say your intention in Arabic and it being just a mouthing of words before you sleep.

Understand what it is that you are intending. Understand that you are giving up. Understand that you are giving up for Allah. For a while you are leaving the issue of when you can eat in Allah's hands. The zahid who has taken this way of looking at life to the extremity will not eat unless somebody gives him some food. He will go for days without food, unless somebody puts food in front of him, he will not eat. There are different ways of expressing this principle. Nabi Ebrahim (a.s.) would not eat unless he had some- body to share his food with. All of these things are the slave saying to the Lord: 'I will only eat at the time that You destined and not in the time that I destined.'

We have been given the capacity to try and take charge, to be majestic, so that we can fail at it. It is only once you have attempted to be of use to yourself and failed at it that you see Allah's plan. Only then can you say *"Subhaanallah."* 'He is in charge, and He does better for me than I can do for myself.' While you are behaving like a predator your life is defined by fear. Your life is defined by lack. 'I have got to get this; I have got to get that.' Your being is hurt and becomes destructive.

When I learn to allow the world to come in as a deer does, then I start seeing. Then I see that Allah does better for me than I can do for myself. My fear is replaced with gratitude and trust. The fruit of the fasting is to polish the heart. It is to cultivate the qualities of gratitude and of trust in the heart.

Gratitude and trust are based on the fact that you with- held for Him and you saw that He gave you better. The only reason He wants us to fail at the attempt of being of any use to ourselves is so we can discover that He in fact had better for us all along.

Look back at your life and you will see that this true. Examine your life; see the pattern in your life. See how Allah has brought you to a place where it would have been impossible for you to have worked it out. It is too complex; there have been too many events. There have been too many things that have happened.

So when you make your niyyah tomorrow morning for the fast, make it with the deliberate intention of; 'Ya Allah, I am going too fast for you, Ya Allah, please accept from me my fast.' Know that you are saying: 'Ya Allah, I am going too fast for You in order to learn giving up, Ya Allah, please make this lesson possible for me, please make this a polishing of my heart, please make this a mechanism whereby I can learn trust, whereby I can learn gratitude and whereby I can learn patience.'

Allah says in Surah Al 'Asr **60** "By time, verily man is at a complete loss." In the face of time whatever you think that you could do for yourself that might be useful is utterly futile. You want to get the car, think a bit ahead after you have gained the car.**61** So you get the car and 3 months later somebody steals the car and then you are miserable.

Whatever it is that you think that you can achieve for yourself, because it is temporary, is going to be a source of misery to you. Whatever it is. 'By time', by the fact that things are transient we are at a complete loss. Whatever it is that we do in our own favour rots in our hands. "Except those who believe..." Except those who accept that they are not in charge. "And those who do good deeds."

In the Qur'an these two attributes of 'Amanu wa amilu salihat' are always connected. Believing and doing good work. Doing good work means being patient. It means not doing what you want but doing what is the right thing to do. When you do what is the right thing to do the result is ultimately better than it would have been if you acted on what you wanted.

That only happens when you assume that Allah is in charge in the first place. So 'amanu' is absolutely the root condition of 'amilu salihat'. If you do not believe that Allah is in charge then you are going to take charge and act in your own interests. What is really important about being a Muslim is that the issue does not stop with belief and good works, it goes further. It is to 'encourage others to truth and to encourage others to patience.'

It is not good enough for you to be inwardly correct, or to believe, and to be outwardly correct, or to do good deeds. You have to encourage others to the same. It is a transactional thing. Encouraging others does not just mean that you jabber in Arabic to other Muslims. These are the personal truths, which are the inheritance of all of mankind. You have to exhort others to believing in the good auspices of Being and to being patient in the pursuit of their own interests.

So the fast is an exercise in patience. It is an exercise in 'amilu salihaat'. You do the right thing and Allah elevates your heart. It is very interesting that in the Nguni languages, the word for believe and the word for trust are the same word. Ukuthemba. Now that is fascinating.

To believe is to trust. It is the same reality. How do you trust? By ceasing to believe that you are useful to yourself.

May Allah grant us success on the path.
May Allah grant us nearness to Him.
May Allah grant us annihilation in Him.
May Allah grant us death before we die.

Al Hamdulillah.

———

59: A.A. - If we don't pursue it and discover the anti-climax, we will continue to be obsessed by it. It has to be tried.

60: The Qur'an: *"By Time.*

Verily, man is in a state of loss. Except those who believe, and those who do good deeds, and encourage others to the truth and encourage others to patience." [103:1-3].

61: T.S. - Not that there's anything wrong with wantinga car as long as you don't think that getting it will be the cure for all your ills/feelings of lack, or that you don't consume yourself with the desire for it. If you are consumed with the desire for it, either get one or imagine all the consequences of having one.

Listen!
Discourse 16: 9th February, 2001

Bismillahir Rahmanir Rahim:

There are two principal senses that allow the world into our being, our sight and our hearing. You can disable a person's touch and you can disable a person's smell and taste, and they will probably still be able to function. But a human being is extremely compromised if he does not see and if he does not hear. In most Bantu languages the word for hearing, tasting, smelling and feeling is the same word. In Zulu, for example it is 'ukuzwa', which means to sense. The same word is used for all of these senses. However, sight is perceived as being different.

So really, there are two principal ways in which we experience the world. It is seeing, and that which we sense other than seeing. Now, people normally function on the basis of appearances. In other words, we principally experience life through our sight. Most people work like that. When we say that things are not what they appear to be, or that things are not as they seem, the first significance of that is that behind the apparition, which is about sight, is a deeper reality.

We also know that to be looked at, and to be listened to, are two very different experiences. In the days before you were Muslim, and you were sitting in a pub, and someone was looking at you, this could very easily have turned into a fight. 'What are you looking at?' being the phrase that starts all the trouble. To feel that somebody is looking at you is intrusive. Their eyes penetrate your being.

However; if you sense that somebody is listening to you, there is a completely different transaction that is taking place. You feel far more comfortable being listened to than being looked at. Somebody looks at you and you feel that they are intruding into you. If somebody is listening to you, it actually means that you are going into him or her. There is receptiveness about listening.

So, these two senses, looking and listening, function in two very different ways. Listening is also associated with language. Language is that which conveys meaning, and we know that meaning is never outside of the thing, you know. What makes one signpost different from another is that it indicates something else. It has a different symbol in it. In other words, it is more than it appears to be. It is not just the object, the object has something inside, and that is meaning. In other words, things are not as they appear, they have meaning. There is something deeper going on in it. This meaning becomes apparent by sensing other than seeing. It is something which is missed when you are only looking.

If somebody speaks to you, you hear him or her. You hear the significance of what they are trying to say, the meaning of what they are saying. The objective noise carries a meaning inside, and the meaning is not the sound. Sight, more than any other sense, reduces everything to objects; to an externality without an inside. It is the first sense, if you like, of the materialistic way of looking at things. Sight deals with the outside, with appearance, not with the inside or meaning.

Listening is the sense we associate with language. It is the sense of meaning. It is that which is beyond the apparition and the appearance.**38** Now, it is very interesting that the very first Surah that was revealed to the Beloved Prophet (s.a.w.s.) instructed him *"Read, read in the name of your Lord who made you from a clot of blood"*.**39** When we read we are using the eye, but in a different way to what we do when we are looking. Reading text and looking at objects are very different uses of the eye. Reading turns what the eye sees as objects into signs that carry meaning. Reading is the eye's way of hearing. It is turning the eye into a receptive sense organ, like the ear.

Look at a person who is reading a piece of text and you may see that their lips are moving. What are they doing? They are repeating to themselves that which they are reading. In other words, they are turning what they are seeing into a deeper thing, into language. In other words, what Allah is telling us in this Surah is not just to look at things, but to read them and therefore to see that which is behind what appears to be. See the meaning of the event. This enables you to turn your looking into listening.

The Beloved Rasul (s.a.w.s.) said that he loved three things dearly; he loved women, perfume and the coolness of his eye in prayer. What an extraordinary expression. The coolness of one's eye. A hot eye is an eye that radiates. A hot eye is an eye that intrudes, that is desirous, and that wants things. A man that has no manners will walk into the company of women and look at them, look at them with an eye that says; 'I want you.' This is intrusive, it is disrespectful and discourteous.

A man that is courteous will have soft eye contact, and will not be intrusive, he will not stare the other person down. He will give the person his ear; he will listen to him. In other words, he will not try to see what will be in that interaction for him to get the other person to give him what he wants. His attention, his eye is not going to be focussed on what he wants. He will switch that off and open his attention up so that the other person can announce to him what they want, what they are about, and what their issue is about.

So a cool eye is an eye that does not radiate, or have a desire. It is therefore an eye which is reflective, which is soft, which is about reading and understanding the significance, rather than looking at the other from the point of view of achieving your best advantage.

We have discussed this on a number of occasions: If you want something from somebody else, their ability to withhold what you want makes you manipulable. In other words, your attention is on the other in terms of what the other can give you. Your being is sucked out towards the other. The woman has what I want; the man has what I want, whatever. Your eyes are on that thing. You are looking at what you want, and your being and your attention expresses your desire.

This is what Shaykh Ali Al Jamal referred to as outward gatheredness. Your being is gathered towards the other. Outward gatheredness comes at a price though, and that is inner separation. If your attention is caught up in what you want from the world, you become a stranger to your own heart; you become a strange to your own quiet inside.

To the spacelessness, limitlessness and vastness which is at the centre of your being. Shaykh Ali Al Jamal also said that if you are inwardly gathered, you will be outwardly separated. In other words, if you withdraw your attention from its occupied state in the world, and you return it to its rightful place behind your eyes, you separate from the world, and you find your own inner depth. You take back your territory.

This is absolutely connected with the whole issue of a cool eye. An eye that looks on the world without penetrating, without wishing to dominate; without wishing to achieve some outcome beneficial to you, is an eye which is soft and cool. We get taught in this barbaric system that we are in that we have to be like John Wayne. That we have to look somebody in the eye until he turns to a pool of wobbling jelly. We are taught that this is what it means to be a man, to be strong. All that it proves is that you are a brute. It is discourteous; it ignores the deeper issues associated with being you. This is not culturally specific. If a culture encourages brutal eye contact, it will be based on doing violence to the other. It will be competitive, and it will be vicious. This competitiveness eventually creates a 'dog eat dog' social world which is fundamentally self-destructive over time. It is an aberration of humanness, it is not human, it is not correct, and it is discourteous.

That does not mean to say that you should be shifty, but it means that when you are interacting with people you give them your ear before you give them your eye. You listen to them intently. It might mean that you look at the person but what happens is that from your eye to them becomes a very different transaction. It is no longer confrontative.

Allah tells us *"Read!"*, tells us to look at the world around us with the understanding that things are not as they seem, because He has made us from a clot of blood.**40** You know, human beings are the most extraordinary creatures, which can think, compose poetry, write music, sing, build buildings and send rockets into orbit. This extraordinary being comes from that which is despicable, dirty and blameworthy; a clot of blood. Subhaanallah. That which appears completely insignificant is actually the khalif of existence.

So, things are not as they seem. Don't judge a book by its cover or a clot of blood by its lowliness. Everything is something else; everything is different to what it appears to be. Things are always more than they appear to be. So don't just take it as you see it, use your eye when you interact with the world as a reading tool. Don't just look at it, listen to it, and hear it. Stop trying to penetrate the world, allow the world to penetrate you. Let it into your being. Allow it in. How can you be ravished by the beauty and the majesty that He sets before you when you remain the despoiler? (These are two different transactions.)

We are all going to die, sooner than we think. It is always a surprise when it comes. The last thing my father said to me in the last conversation we had was 'It feels like yesterday that I was a boy. My life has gone in a flash'. He was then a man of 74. Two weeks later he was dead.

There will be a time when our eyes will not see, when we will lose consciousness, when all that we have is the vastness that is behind our eyes, on the inner-side of our being. If this has not become occupied territory, it will be a wilderness for you; it will be a place of hell. So, rescue your attention and put it back into your being. Make your own inner world an occupied place; do not make it foreign territory. Do not allow it to be wild. Do not allow it to be Jehannam, a place defiled by unresolved needs, desires and expectations; a place that consumes.

We have the technology to do this, and that technology is the practice of our deen. All the practices of our deen tell us what the first Revelation told our Nabi (s.a.w.s.); they tell us to shut-up, and listen. Stop looking, stop trying to work it out, stop trying to manage the affair, stop trying to get the angle, to work out your best advantage. Stop trying to be in control and to be in charge.

Listen very astutely, very carefully to what Allah is asking of you now. You have to look deeper than just the appearance of the matter. You have to look with an eye that is an ear; you have to look with the intention to read the meaning inside, to allow the meaning which is in the object to come into your being. One of the marks of realized beings is that they have the extraordinary capacity to see through you. Now, that is not because their eyes penetrate you, it is because you spill out of yourself. All they do, is they let you in. It is not that they are invading you; it is rather you are occupying them and making it quite clear to them what you are actually about. They no longer see the appearance, they read the text.

Every moment that faces you has new meaning, it has a deeper significance, and that significance is always higher, of a higher order than the appearance of the thing. The meaning of the thing is always deeper and more wonderful than the actual outer shell, than the appearance of it. This is so by necessity, because the meaning is real and the appearance is appearance. It is arbitrary. This means to say that if you occupy a world which you are allowing in and listening to, the world that you occupy is by definition a richer place to be. It is a place where you experience and see far more richness than you could ever imagine. **41**

May Allah grant us a cool eye.

May He grant us an openness of the ear.

May He grant us the skill to listen.

May Allah grant us the ability to allow the other to announce themselves.

May Allah grant us respectful eye contact.

May He grant us courtesy in our interaction with others.

May Allah create the conditions where we do not wish to dominate the others with our eyeing.

May Allah bless our beloved Prophet Muhammad, and his family and his companions and the transmitters who have carried his heart to us over the centuries.

Al Hamdulillah.

38: F.A. - Hearing is the first sense we develop/are granted - and also the last sense we lose (i.e. Qur'anic reference to the 'Last Trumpet'.) This shows the significance of hearing.

39: The Qur'an: [96:1-2].

40: The Qur'an: *"Read: In the name of thy Lord who createth. Createth man from a clot."* [96:1- 2]

41: F.A. - *"What we achieveinwardly will changeouter reality."* -Greek author Plutarch.

Submission and Witnessing
Discourse 17: 6th July, 2001

Bismillahir Rahmanir Rahim:

Allah says that He will forgive us anything except shirk.**42** He will forgive your murder, your adultery, your abuse of money, and your theft; He will forgive you all of these things, except for your claim to partnership with Him. On the basis of this, most people, whether they are Muslim or kafir, are worse than the lowest murderers, because most people spend their lives making things other than Allah significant.

Most of us have an idea of wanting to succeed at this project of our lives, and we define this success as being based on something that we can do. We view success as an achievement; it is the outcome of doing all the right things. It is based on manipulating a set of events that will have an outcome beneficial to ourselves.

This illusion that you can manipulate a set of events to gain a beneficial outcome for yourself is a claiming of the capacity to manage the affair, which is an aspect of shirk. If there is only One Actor, then you are not the actor, you are the witness. Fundamentally, Allah did not make you to act, He made you to witness. He made you to witness that He is in charge.

Allah says that the only reason why He made existence is because He loved to be known. He did not create existence so that we could build madrassa's and masjid's, and have intelligent discussions about the deen, about energy fields, or about how to heal the human condition. This is all just a shadow-show, it is a play. All of these activities are ways of dancing with the Great Choreographer, the Great Scripter of all things. If they are not seen in this light, then they are shirk.

Allah also says that there is nothing He loves more than the tauba of a sinner, of somebody who has transgressed. A person who has transgressed and recognizes that he has transgressed is at the point of giving up. He is saying: 'I have messed it up; I took charge and now look at what I have done. Just look at what this life of mine has turned into, it is a mess.'

That is the station in which Allah wants us. That person is in a higher state than the so-called pious person who has laid up his little account for akhira because he has done his salah five times a day and he has averted his eyes from the pretty girl and he has done all of these good things. To do this is to presume that you are able to be of benefit to yourself.43 There is no benefit from any source other than Him. Action is by its intention. When action is founded on an investment in the houri's of the Jannat then this is not un- conditional action. It is not the action of the one who is in awe and worshipful. It is the action of a merchant or trader. In reality, we cannot be of benefit to ourselves.

One of the implications of this is the miracle that Allah consistently calls forth blessing from our failure. **Allah will turn even the worst and the ugliest things about your life, into a blessing**. Allah is the Great Transformer; He is the Great Miracle Maker. He made the whole of the universe from nothing. He makes some- thing from emptiness, he makes blessing from curse. He can turn one thing into another. He is the Transformer.

This is one of the significances of istighfaar. Istighfaar means that by disavowing, by handing over, by saying: 'Cover me, I have messed it up, You take over, cover me, take charge.' By you saying that , the conditions are created where He transforms the ill into a blessing.44 I have mentioned here before that one of the most extraordinary people that I have ever met was Imam Gafielien, the Imam of the Bosmont Mosque. He had the unenviable task of being the only Muslim cleric who was prepared to serve as chaplain in the days of apartheid for the Muslims' executions.

He would work with the individuals before their execution. He would walk with them on that last walk to the trapdoor; he would stand with the men as they fell through the hole. He told me that what he found most remarkable about all these men was that it did not matter how evil the man was, and what he was being executed for, (and some of these individuals were guilty of the most staggering crimes), on that last walk, in those last five minutes, they all became as meek as lambs. They would turn to their jailers and the people around them and thank them. They displayed only the highest courtesy in their final minutes.

You see, if you know the proximity of death, if you are looking it straight in the eye, you cannot be self-important. You can only be in your rightful place, which is to be meek, kind, and merciful; to be gentle with the people around you. That is giving up, that is handing over and that is submission, Islam.

That giving up turns the crime that led him down the passage towards the execution chamber into part of his blessing. He would not have had that moment of conscious and deliberate handing over if he had not committed that horrendous crime that had brought him to that place. So the blessing is precisely that set of events that took place. The murder and the mayhem that he had caused was a part of the opening of the gates of Jannat for him.

So, who is to judge? Who are we to judge people? Who is to say that the very worst thing that you have done in your life is not going to turn out to be the biggest opening for you? To be the opening of your biggest blessing. Who is to say that the most holy thing that you have done in your life is not going to turn out to be the biggest millstone around your neck, which will drag you to the deepest pit of Jehannam, because it was done as a self conscious and presumptuous act of piety.

You are not to say. Allah tells us in a hadith al qudsi that you can behave your entire life like a person from the garden. You can do good acts, and in the last minutes of your life, you can behave like a person from the fire and you will go to the fire. Subhaanallah. And then he said that you can behave your entire life like a person from the fire, and in the last moments of your breath you can behave like a person from the garden, and then you will go to the garden.

This is Allah's transformative capacity. That transformative capacity is based on the most subtle thing in your core, which is: do you or do you not accept that Allah is in charge? If you accept that He is in charge within your deepest core, and you take your hands off the steering wheel of your life, He will turn everything into blessing, the good and the bad.

If you try to put your hands on the steering wheel of this life of yours and try to take charge, He will turn everything about you into a curse, the good and the bad.**45**

So, you are indeed blessed to live in a theatre of miracles where that which is terrible becomes that which is wonderful, and where that which our ego pursues as wonderful becomes terrible. Subhaanallah. This is part of what Shaykh Ali Al Jamal means when he says 'The meaning of the thing is hidden in its opposite'. I had a most intriguing discussion with Shaykh Fadhlallah a couple of weeks ago. We were driving in the car when he said;

'You know, you have got to accept everything on face value. You have got to accept that it is all from Allah and do not judge it. You have got to be open. Believe everything.' I replied, 'Yes, yes, yes, Shaykh Fadhlallah' as if I understood, at least I thought I had understood. We were driving on for a little while when he said: 'No, no, no, no, you must believe nothing'

He had said exactly the opposite! But life is exactly like that. Do not be presumptuous, do not be presumptuous. Accept absolutely everything at face value; accept absolutely nothing at face value. Know that the thing is always more than it appears to be. Nothing is as it seems. Everything is bigger than it presents itself as being, every single thing.

Every moment which Allah gives you has in it a potential that is bigger than you can calculate, see, or apprehend. It appears to be just another moment, but it is a coming together of the miraculous. If you accept that this is the case, which by His Rahmat He will turn that which is in front of you into something stupendous, it will become something stupendous. As Shaykh Fadhlallah says: 'You will be amazed, you will be amazed, you will be amazed.' Every moment will be something astonishing.

If you appraise the moment in front of you on the basis of your narrow-mindedness, and on the basis of your presumptions, of what you think it is all about, then all you will have is the appearance. You will not find the depth behind it; you will not have the other possibility. Then all you see is your assumption of it. Allah says that He is in his slaves' expectations of Him. So, He presents to you your expectation.

A key survival skill to cultivate in our time is to be like a frightened child in the company of its mother. A timid child, that when you stray a little bit from Allah, you very quickly run back, clinging on, and saying: 'I do not understand, this is too big for me, I am frightened, You take over, I cannot, I am not in charge of it.' The more you do that, the more you will see things open up to you which will leave you silent and speechless with awe.

This status of being silent and speechless with awe is the reason we were created in the first place. This is the only reason we have been made. It is to cotton on to and experience that moment of awe. Anything but that moment is a waste of your time. It is an absolute waste of your life. Anything less than awe is not doing with your life what it has been designed to do. You do not use a rifle to dig a hole. You do not use a knife to chisel into concrete. You do not use a pair of knitting needles to cook a piece of meat. You use the right thing for its right purpose.**46**

You, as the pinnacle of creation, have been created for one reason only, and that reason is to be astonished at the Creator of this creation. It is the only reason why you have been made. Everything that you do, other than that, is a misapplication of your life and is self-destructive. So, all of the projects are fine, when they are dealt with in play. That goes for all your projects, your business, family, and the struggle for Africa that has just started.

All the nonsense that has happened up to this moment was just the writing of the preface of the book of your life. None of these things are worthwhile engaging in if you are going to lose yourself in the process. They are only worthwhile engaging in if they are the means you use in order to see Allah at work. You can work like that, you can take on any task or any activity from the point of view of being able to see how Allah makes His creation and puts it together, in order for you to witness.

You can take on any task from the point of view of emptying yourself so that you can become His vessel. When you achieve this, it is no longer you who are acting, it is Him acting. You can dance like that, you can sing like that, you can write a poem like that, you can conduct business like that, you can sail a boat like that, and you can slaughter a cow like that.

From one point of view the blessing of the sunnah is to provide us with the technology whereby we can do this in our day to day lives; whereby our day to day lives can be a constant handing over and giving up to Allah. Every single activity is engaged deliberately from the point of view of giving up, of being Muslim, of submitting. How you eat your food, how you brush your teeth, how you deport yourself in the toilet and how you deal with your spouse, all of these things are opportunities to submit and witness. The reason why the sunnah is there, is to show us that we can be submitting beings in this world without losing our connection to it.

May Allah make us people of submission.
May Allah make us people of kindness.
May Allah cure our rancour.
May Allah relieve us of the illusions that we can do better for ourselves than what He can do for us.
May Allah grant us nearness to Him.
May Allah grant us annihilation in Him.
May Allah grant us death before we die.

Al Hamdulillah.

42: F.A. - The Qur'an: *"Lo! Allah forgiveth not that a partner should be ascribed unto Him. He forgiveth (all) save that to whom He will. Whoso ascribeth partners to Allah, he hath indeed invented a tremendous sin."* [4:48]. Also: *"...nor does He share His command with anyone whatsoever."* [18:26].

43: T.S. - This doesn'tmean you can do what you want and feel fine because you'll be forgiven - actions are judged by intentions. It is your intention you have to watch! 'Why am I doing this?'

44: T.S. - Assuming that you are sincere.

45: T.S. - This is not passivity, it means watching for what is needed from you in the situation, at that time, and acting or refraining from action accordingly; not acting according to what you want out of the situation you are in.

46: F.A. - Your life is to be used to witnessHim.

Expansion and Contraction: It's like breathing

Discourse 18: 20th July, 2001

Bismillahir Rahmanir Rahim:

I once heard Shaykh Abdal Qadir narrate an experience that he had in Morocco while he was a mureed of Shaykh Muhammad Ibn al Habib. This experience centred on the theme of glorifying Allah and of giving praise to Him, Al Hamdulillah. He said that he was sitting in the zawia of Shaykh Muhammad Ibn al Habib with a group of fuqara when he got news of some good fortune which had befallen him and he was so delighted, that he said *"Al Hamdulillah."*

One of the older fuqara in the circle looked at him completely shocked as if he had said something rude. He held Shaykh Abdal Qadir's hand and said very deliberately, articulating very slowly: *"Yes, Al Hamdulillah. Al Hamdulillah."* This disturbed Shaykh Abdal Qadir because he did not know what the man meant. Sometime later they were sitting in the circle again when the same faqir received news that all three of his sons had just been killed in a car crash. The man sat back, closed his eyes and just said *"Al Hamdulil- lah. Al Hamdulillah."* That was all anyone could get out of that man for the rest of the evening *"Al Hamdulillah."* Then Shaykh Abdal Qadir realized what the man had been trying to tell him.

To flippantly just say: 'Al Hamdulillah.' when things are going well is to be stupid, vain, shallow and frivolous, because unless you are prepared to praise Allah by His names of Majesty, you have not got the right to praise Him by His names of Beauty. We are all very quick to say; 'Al Hamdulillah.' when things go well and to our reckoning.

We forget however to say; 'Al Hamdulillah' when things go badly and not to our reckoning. We seek to get out of the constrictions as soon as possible. We do not realize that those times are in fact our best times and that the times where we think that things are going very well, those are actually the times when we are in danger.

The way of Allah is expansion and contraction. There is a summer and there is a winter. There is ebb and there is a flow. There is rest and then there is activity. To praise Allah just when things are exciting, when there is activity and expansion and to get depressed when there is contraction, is not recognizing Allah's way. It also doubts Allah. It doubts Allah's promise. His promise to us is that whatever He gives us is for our own benefit. His promise to us is that if you are on the right path and you are sincere, then whatever He takes away from you, He takes away for one reason only, and that is so that He can give back to you that which is better. You cannot have the higher if you still hold onto the lower. So, every time that we are in loss or constriction we should say; *"Al Hamdulillah."* in good faith that Allah is using this as an opportunity to grant us something more.

Shaykh Ali Al Jamal says that the meaning of the thing is in its opposite. This means that when you are expanded outwardly, you are actually inwardly contracted, and restricted. When you are restricted outwardly (are confined) or Allah's names of Majesty are being visited upon you outwardly; you have inner expansion.

If you are in the hurly-burly of the successful trade in the marketplace you do not remember that there is this infinity. You forget the sea of bliss behind your eyes, which you have instant access to, because the excitement of being in the hurly-burly is just too enchanting and too structured.

This means that we need to have our access to the hurly-burly constricted, to constrict the excitement of outer success. We need it to be contained so that an inner depth can develop. Shaykh Ali Al Jamal says that if you are outwardly gathered, you will be inwardly separate. If your attention is trapped in the world then you are alien to your own nature. You do not know who you are. If you are inwardly gathered, you will be outwardly separate. This means that if you have befriended your own nature, if you are gathered to your inner core, the other has no hold over you. You are separate from the other.

The other can ebb and can flow and it is all; 'Al Hamdulillah. Al Hamdulillah.' You do not get stupid and superficial about your assessment of success and failure. You develop, as the path continues, with the curiosity of a child, knowing that every day there will be something else which is going to be amazing. That something else which is going to be amazing can only be announced to you and can only become apparent to you if you are looking at life with an unjaundiced eye; with an eye that is not trying to fulfil the self's expectations of life.

Your expectations are only value judgements, concerned with rule of thumb assessments that judge this as good and that as bad. This is positive and that is negative. This is praiseworthy and that is blameworthy. Who is to say? Who is to say what is praiseworthy and what is blameworthy? Out of the excrement there comes lettuce. Out of the lettuce there comes excrement. Al Hamdulillah.

We are so quick to judge and walk around as if we are the one and only judge, jury and executioner of existence, as if existence depends on us to denote its significance and its importance. By doing this, all we are doing is looking into the filters of our own presumption. We are not seeing existence as it really is. If we saw existence as it really was, we would not demean anything. We would see that everything has its place and that everything comes from Allah. We would treat everything with the proper courtesy. You treat the fertilizer with courtesy because treating it with courtesy means that you recognize that from the fertilizer comes your food.

This propensity to judge, to get caught up in our inner noise of weighing up, evaluating and valuing everything is the greatest stumbling block on the path. Your propensity to judge is also an aspect of shirk. It is about wanting to manage the outcome of affairs. Managing the outcome of affairs depends on things being judged as helpful or harmful to your agenda. This means that you reduce things to your own presumption about their merit.

I will give you an example of this. Let us say that you have had three bad experiences with Lebanese people in your life. They all cheated you. The fourth Lebanese that you meet is actually quite a sensible fellow and he does not want to cheat you. However, you buy something from him and when he gives you your change, he has short-changed you. Now, the man has made a genuine mistake, but because you presume that all

Lebanese people are cheats, this man has just confirmed your presumption of Lebanese people.

You are likely to treat the fifth Lebanese that you meet as a thief. He sees your distrustful behaviour (due to the fourth man) and he assumes that you must have something to hide. He experiences you as potentially dangerous, so he starts to respond to you in a suspicious way which again just confirms your belief that he is a thief.

We set up the world around us on the basis of our own presumptions. In the meantime only three of the Lebanese people are bad and it happened to be the first three which you met. The rest of the Lebanese people were perfectly wonderful. In fact, the other three who were particularly bad just happened to be bad at the time when you met them. **47**

You see, you have not lived very long if you do not recognise that a person is not the same creature when he goes to bed at night as he was in the morning. For example, in the morning, this person, well he is just not a morning person. In the morning he is grouchy and irritable. So you meet him in the morning and you think; 'What an awful person this is.' If you had met this same person at night you would have said; 'What a wonderful person this man is.'

Somebody else might be exactly the opposite. The man is a morning person and you meet him in the morning when he is all sunshine. You think that he is a wonderful man. You meet the same man in the afternoon and you would probably think that he is a monster.

You cannot say that a person is such and such, or he is like this or that. You have not lived very long if you think like that. You are not being truthful to your own experience of life. All people can and do change. Their existence changes and it changes moment by moment in the most breathtaking ways. We do not recognise and allow the change because we keep on assuming that we think that we know it all.**48**

The reason why we have been created is so we can discover that we actually know nothing. So that we can discover that whatever our knowledge of existence is, it is in fact very faulty. Knowledge belongs only to Allah, not to you. If you think that you know, then you really do not know at all. You have only made a judgement of a thing, 'it is like this, and it is like that'. The only thing that you have demonstrated is your own stupidity. Allah is the only One who knows.

His knowledge is the knowledge of ambivalence, of opposites, of the subtle, and of what we cannot define.**49**

He is the One Who brings life from death. He is the One Who brings death from life. You can look at the corpse - this thing is thoroughly dead, it is rotting, and Allah will bring life out of that. You can look at the man walking down the road today, he is healthy and he is perfectly fine. You wonder how it is possible that this man can die, become smelly and rotten. Tonight a spider bites him in his bed and by tomorrow morning he is dead. How on earth is that possible? Because today the man is dead, does that mean that he was not alive yesterday?

So this is the significance of what Shaykh Fadhlallah said to me a couple of months ago when he said; 'Treat absolutely everything on face value, believe everything and believe nothing.' This means that you cannot judge anything. Allow the world to surprise you, because when you do the world does surprise you. When you open your self to the possibilities Allah demonstrates just how in charge He really is. He will demonstrate to you just how surprising He really is and how amazing His way really is.

Allah has created the whole of existence as a theatre so that He can show you surprise upon surprise, wonder upon wonder. It is as if He says to us 'Now what do you think about this? And this? And this?' The only reason you exist is for that awe. You have no other purpose. You have no purpose other than to praise Allah and to bear witness that He is indeed the Most Praiseworthy, The Most High.

How can you praise Allah if you keep on being judgmental about His theatre? This whole sweep of existence and all the people who come and go in and out of our lives, the only reason why it happens, is so that we can see how amazing Allah really is. When you keep on disapproving of His theatre by which He presents His show to you, you have to be displaying an attribute of the most breathtaking arrogance.

So when somebody comes to you and you see that this is a cheating Lebanese, then say; *"Al Hamdulillah."* Because from him might come a flower. From the fertilizer comes the beauty. From Allah only extraordinary things come, and all things come from Him. Allow it to come. Do not try to freeze it to your own presumptions, or as they say in Afrikaans; *"Hy is so gemaak en so gelaat staan."* In other words, he has been made like that and he was left like that. This is not how things work. Nothing is like that. You are not like that.

Are you the same person who you were twenty years ago? Of course you are not. Not even the atomic material of your body is still the same. Your entire physical structure gets replaced within a very short period of time. You are not even physically the same being. The atoms, which were inside the form of your body eighteen months ago, are no longer there.

So who is to say that you are such and such, and that you are so and so? The more you can understand this about existence the more you will understand this about yourself. This is what freedom really means. Freedom really means that you are not presumptuous about your own nature. Freedom means that you recognize that you have the whole of existence within you. From the worst to the best.

The understanding we have that a person has the potential to become the worst devil and rise to the highest angel, is not just sequentially true, it is simultaneously true. In any given moment you can actualise the angelic and the diabolical, because they are both present in you. You actually have the whole menagerie of existence inside of you.

You have the whole thing. You have within you a donkey. You have within you a dog. You have within you a shark. You have within you a piranha, a cockatoo, an orangutan, whatever, it is all there. You have within you all of the minerals, you have within you all of the vegetables. You are in actual fact a carbon copy of the whole of existence.

So when you disapprove of something in existence, you are disapproving of something within yourself. When you are limiting something in existence, you are limiting yourself. As you are with the world, so the world is with you. We know this. The person who is at war with the Lebanese has the Lebanese at war with him. Not only that, but because the Lebanese are inside him as much as outside him he is actually at war against himself.

A person who disapproves of something is actually disapproving of himself. That does not mean he is an idiot who cannot, or does not stop the thief when he sees the thief. When it is in his power to exercise the shariah by cutting the thief's hand off, he does so. He does all these things, but he does them with a free heart. He does it without judgement. He does it with no disapproval. He does not burden himself with the responsibility of pronouncing judgement on existence all the time.

There is another beautiful saying in Afrikaans, which goes; *"Moet nie 'n moordkuil van jou hart maak nie."* In other words, 'Do not make a place of murder inside of your heart.' If something affects you or if something afflicts you, say 'Al Hamdulillah, I know that there is a blessing in this; I just cannot see it right now.' How else can you deal with anything which goes wrong? You see somebody who is behaving like an absolute swine, say; 'Al Hamdulillah, I know that in this there is some kind of a blessing, I just cannot see it right now. Maybe the blessing is that I will have the joy of giving him a clout, Al Hamdulillah.'

You do not carry this burden of disapproval around with you all the time. You do not twist your heart. You have a heart that knows that all of this has been scripted for you, and that it is for your benefit. All the good and all the bad. Your highest benefit is that moment of surprise when you see the Hand of Allah; the moment you can truly say; *"Al Hamdulillah."* Irrespective of what the event was. A person who can do that is free. They are free because they have been unconditional. They have been unconditional because they have been unconditioned. Creation has no power over them.

We know from Shaykh Ali Al Jamal that if you are safe from yourself, then you are safe from existence. If you are at war with yourself, then you are at war with existence. It is exactly the same theme as; 'Disapprove of the world and you are disapproving of yourself.' This is how people become sick. This is how people get cancer. This is how people die. All the twistedness; it is all because they think that they know better than life. They want to dominate life. They want to control life. Unfortunately they are picking an opponent which is somewhat bigger than them. Allah will take them on in terms of the subtlest dynamics of their being. Allah will destroy them with those dynamics. We make plans and He makes plans and He is the best of planners.

May Allah grant us success on the path.
May Allah grant us nearness to him.
May Allah grant us annihilation in Him.
May Allah grant us death before we die.

Al Hamdulillah.

———

47: F.A. - People are dynamic - failing to recognize that people are consistently changing and that they are seldom the same throughout the day, let alone a lifetime; is naïve.

48: F.A. - We do not recognise the change because we continue to displace it with our assumption that we know it all.

49: T.S. - This could be taken as being nihilistic, particularly by young people. However, it isn't actually, as you'll see if you read it carefully. It is not a reason not to act or seek knowledge. Differentiate between levels. Early in the journey, the difference will be mostly theoretical. Later, finer differentiation becomes possible. Do what is appropriate for your situation at the time. Act, but recognise where the true knowledge and significance lies.

LOVE
Discourse 25: 24th November, 2000

Bismillahir Rahmanir Rahim:

We know that Allah Subhanahu wa ta'ala is outwardly manifested. This suggests that the Totality of the Other which wraps around you is Him. Now, the first implication of this is that He observes you from every possible angle. There is nothing that you can do, or think, or say, or intend, which is outside of His reach. Given the fact that we are designed and required to live our lives in worship of Allah; if we are not worshipping, we are acting in a way contrary to His design for us, and His requirement of us for our lives.

This act of rebellion or contrariness is witnessed most intimately. He sees that, and what is interesting, is that despite the fact that we act on the basis of intention and attitude which is not consistent with His requirement of us, He does not annihilate us with one blow. This can only suggest that Allah owns patience, as He owns love. The entire story of creation is a story of long suffering, patience, tolerance, kindness and mercy. The whole story of existence is a story of love.

He has shaped every one of us, and He has made us the way that we are, so that we can make the very particular contribution that we are called to make. This means to say that He knows you better than you know yourself. He watches over you every moment that you are alive. He sees what is coming beyond the moment. He sees what is hidden in the breasts of people around you. He sees it all, and He has your very best interest as the centre of His concern.

He has made you to worship Him, which means that Allah has an intimate interest in each of us. Allah is not a big fellow sitting in the sky with a big beard, disconnected from your everyday life. He is immediate. He is present. Not only is He present, but He is present in a way which has your very best interests in mind. Allah is concerned with developing the highest aspects in you, and the highest aspect in you is the worshipping of Him. He has fashioned you to perfection, for Him.

Your physiology, your biography, your struggles have all been part of the journey to shape your life into the perfect platform for your unique vantage point; your unique place for witnessing Him. He has a greater interest in the fulfilment of the purpose of your life than you have. Everything that happens to you has a core agenda of creating the conditions where you deliberately and with intention submit to Him. He is busy leading you to the higher purpose of your life. He is already more capably in charge of your life than you are.

There is an account of the Rasul (s.a.w.s.) before the battle of Badr. He was confronted by a kafir who was about to impale him with his sword. The kafir said to the Rasul (s.a.w.s.) *"And who is going to protect you now?"* The Rasul (s.a.w.s.) responded: *"Allah will protect me."* The kafir was so astonished at this response that he dropped his sword and surrendered to the Rasul (s.a.w.s.).

We understand that we have to tie the camel, but make no mistake; if Allah wishes you injury there is no amount of protection and security in the world that will keep you safe. Conversely, if Allah wishes you safety, there is no amount of threat in the world that can injure you. That is how it is. In essence, the fact that you are still alive, the fact that Allah still tolerates everyone, all of us, with our silliness, our pettiness, and our muddled intentions, indicates Allah's benevolent intent toward us.

Allah has not annihilated you yet. This, by definition means that your purpose is not yet played out. He still has a role for you. That role is concerned with maturing the best in you. What makes it possible for you to act on the basis of His requirement of you, rather than the mediocrity that you are willing to settle for? It is the security of knowing that He is here, that He is watching you, that He is present, and that He is accessible. This trust in Him enables Life to call upon the best in you. It creates the conditions where you can indeed hand over your affair to Him, and not take care of your affair yourself. You cannot do better for yourself than Allah can do for you.

When we are overwhelmed by the complexities of our day to day life it is useful to remember that He is the One who has delivered you to that point. He is the One who will take you out of it. Allah is the One who makes the openings possible. He is the One who brings the closing. You do not have to work it all out; you can afford to entrust the matter to Him because He has your best interest at heart. Allah has your best interests at heart in such a way that by His ingenuity He can make things possible for you that you can never make possible for yourself.

May Allah grant us success on the path
May He grant us nearness to Him
May He grant us annihilation in Him
Allah, grant peace and blessings on our Nabi (s.a.w.s.)

Al Hamdulillah.

HAND OVER TO ALLAH
Discourse 26: 26th January, 2001

Bismillahir Rahmanir Rahim:

In one of the Qur'anic Surah's which Sidi Alaoui recited (Surah An Nasr), Allah warns us that when He opens things for us and people start coming in to the deen in droves, we should not forget Him. Then Allah says that He is the Most Forgiving and the Most Often Returning. This is an extraordinary message. The Surah has historical significance; it indicates that by the help of Allah the Muslims became populous and plentiful. Many people became Muslims, but that very success was in a sense the great point of danger. Hypocrisy or nifaq was not an issue in Makkah, because the Muslims were a persecuted minority. However, nifaq became an increasingly significant issue in Medina, when being Muslim had definite political benefits associated with it.

Further to this, when He grants His help and He allows the opening is when people have a tendency to forget Him. You know you need a Rabb, a guardian Lord, in times of trouble. However, when things are going well we very quickly fall into the trap of feeling self-sufficient.

The deeper significance of this Surah for our lives is not just that there will one day be a re-establishment of the deen, the Muslims will govern and there will be a time of resurgence, insha'Allah. The Surah also has great significance for our day to day lives. We know from the shaykh's, and Shaykh Fadhlallah said this often; when you are outwardly constricted, you are in a good place, and when you are outwardly expanded, watch out. This is a time of danger. This is the time when you get things wrong.

This is so because the structure of success is always the same, it does not matter whether it is to establish the deen, fight a battle, or build a business.

It is the same deep pattern. You start off in failure and you endeavour to succeed to the point of giving up the struggle, and at the point of giving up the struggle, the opening from Allah comes. That is when His help comes. When you have come to the point where you say; 'Yes Allah, I give up, I have done everything that I can, there is nothing more that I can do, I have tried everything.'

This moment of capitulation is the sweetest moment. It is when you have done your best, struggled to your utmost and then handed the matter over to Him because you realize that success is not in your power, that Allah grants you success. That is when a Muslim is at his highest. That is submission. That is what we have been made to experience.

Allah says that He created us to worship Him. Worshipping means that you find Him the only source of significance, the only source of success, the Manager of the affair. In order to affirm Him as the Manager of the affair, you have to disavow your management of the affair. Allah has made us weak so that we can fool about at trying to manage the affair and fail. At this point of failure, when we throw our hands up and say 'You know, there is nothing I can do', we are at our highest. That is what He made us to be. When we are like that, He brings us success.

Consider any project that you really worked at, one that presented you with a block which you struggled at and then suddenly there was an opening. What you will notice in the structure of how that project worked is that you battled and battled and then at some point you finally gave up, and in the giving up the thing changed. It is like pursuing the woman that you love very much. You will chase after her and while you are chasing after her she runs away. The moment you lose interest she comes towards you.

This is exactly how horse whispering works. The horse whisperer is alone with a wild horse in a paddock, and he pursues the horse for a couple of hours, putting all his attention on the horse. The horse's natural inclination is to run away, because it feels threatened. At some point the whisperer deliberately stops pursuing the horse and looks away from the horse. The horse can't stand that. At this point the horse comes toward the man. Good horse whisperers have been know to be able to back a wild mustang and ride it in one day, with no violence or 'breaking', which is normally associated with horse training.

This is how Allah has structured existence. If you do not chase it, it is also not going to happen. You have got to put himma or effort into it. You have got to put yearning into it and then, you have got to give up. You have got to do your best and then you have got to give up. That little stratagem is the magic formula of success.

However, that formula of success has within it the danger that the moment people give up and the success comes they ascribe the success to their own struggle. They do not see that the success is due to the nasr or help of Allah. They do not see it as a fath, an opening from their Lord. That is why it is dangerous.

Your moment of success is also your moment of greatest weakness, because you give up, you say that 'I cannot do this anymore'. It is also the moment of danger, because when Allah gives it to you, you say; 'Ah, look how clever I am, I managed this, I created this', and that is when our downfall comes. When we arrogate the success to ourselves and claim it for ourselves, we are saying 'it is my doing, I did this'. The appropriate response to the situation is awe because you witness the help from your Lord, not to respond with smugness. Where you should be grateful for the opening because you see it as coming from Him, you rather feel that you are entitled to the success because you worked so hard at it. The purpose of an endeavour is that the outcome of endeavour is awe and gratitude, the twin qualities of worship. When you claim the success for yourself the opposite happens, smugness and entitlement. This is why Allah warns us that at the time of opening we should be vigilant. This is the time when it is critical for us to continue praising Him and asking to have our own inadequacy covered.

This is why modesty is so important; I do not mean false modesty, I do not mean thinking that you are really clever, but then sort of making out that you do not particularly want to be seen to think that you are clever. It means to understand that whatever success you are granted is not you. You cannot make anything work. You can only give up trying to make it work, and then it works.

At that moment you are a shahid, a witness. You are seeing the thing as it is. It is very interesting, that word Shahid is also used for the one who dies in jihad. Now, consider the significance of dying in jihad. It means that you struggle to your utmost limit, and then you die. You give up completely.

Being shahid means struggling to your utmost limit, to the point of being completely expended and then giving up. Complete surrender, because a corpse cannot do or achieve anything. That is when you have Paradise. That is when you have supreme success.

Witnessing means that you see Allah's hand in everything that happens. You recognize the Controller behind the event. You see that He is the One who engineers all success and that He is the One who will give you whatever success you want. You struggle and then you hand it over to Him and He gives it to you. He will give you whatever you want, even the haraam, if that is what you want, if that is what you are pursuing. You will have to pay the price afterwards, of course.

So we see, why Allah cautions us in 'Surah An Nasr' not to forget Him when we have success. It is at our time of outward expansion that we are most likely to fall into the trap of arrogance. However, at time of outward constraint you are safe because you know that you are not making it work. You are also careful, because you feel that you have to watch out. You cannot afford to make a mistake.

The moment that you achieve success and you think 'what a clever fellow I am', you think that the rules do not apply to you anymore. You think you are the chosen one who can behave as he likes. That is a very dangerous place to be in because that is when we get up to mischief. We only get up to mischief when we think that we are in charge and invincible; when we think that we have got life and the world under control.

So delegate and dedicate all the time. Hand over the success to Allah. It is not your affair, He gives you the results. All you need to do is to put in the effort. The results are not your problem. This reminds me of the story of Abe. Abe was a very devout man; he used to pray all the time to the Lord that he should be allowed to win the lottery. He prayed passionately and fervently, 12 hours a day, year after year, 'oh Lord, please let me win the lottery'. One day a booming voice from the sky interrupted his prayer.

"*Abe*", the voice said.

"*Yes Lord*" Abe replied.

"*Abe, at least meet me half way, buy a ticket.*"

Allah also says in Surah An Nasr, that He is verily, the Most Oft Returning. This is because Allah knows that you are going to get it wrong. Allah has made us that way. How can you find, if you have not lost? How can you discover if what you are searching for has not been hidden? This is why there is nothing that Allah loves more than the tauba or repentance of somebody who has erred.

In that moment you surrender, you give up. You say 'I am sorry that I messed up', you distance yourself from any significance of success, and from being able to manage the affair. This distancing of oneself from the delusion of being capable is the heart of the matter. If you can cultivate that consciousness, you have the essence of tauba. You have the essence of witnessing, which we are here to do.

Is it not interesting that the Rasul (s.a.w.s.), who is known to be mahsum or faultless, used to do istighfaar frequently. He used to ask Allah to cover him or ask forgiveness from Allah frequently. The model of the perfect human being is the model of one who distances himself from the illusion of capability.

So we are going to struggle and we are going to give up, and in that moment of giving up, there is a sweetness that Allah promises to realize for us. It is He who will make the opening hap- pen for us. Then we again will become stupid and arrogant and say; 'Look at how clever I am.' At this point then Allah says to us 'I will come back to you, just remember Me.' The pattern of existence is perfect in every respect, it is His design. His design is worthy of worship, of witnessing, of being overwhelmed by.

———

May Allah protect us from our essential arrogance.
May Allah keep us steady on the path.
May Allah keep us vigilant.
May Allah keep us loyal to Him.
May Allah make us careful of our pettiness.
May Allah grant us success.
May Allah grant us nearness to Him and annihilation in Him.
May Allah grant us death before we die.
Oh Allah, grant Peace and Blessings on your Messenger, and on his family and his Companions.
Al Hamdulillah.

Who am I?
Discourse 27: Undated

Bismillahir Rahmanir Rahim:

We have very little idea of how powerful we are as beings and how much the world is in fact in our hands. Most of us have a view that we are defined. We think we are defined by our biographies and our past. We think that we are defined by our history and by the world that we are in. That is only true for you up to a certain point in your development. There comes a point in your development that you are no longer defined by your biography but that you are the one who defines your biography.

To give you an example of this; if you ask any person to choose a number of events that they think are the critical events of their lives; the events that they think really make up who they are; you will find one person writing up a story choosing events that are all about loss and heartache. You will find another person choosing events that are all about rape and abuse. A third person will choose events that are all about success. A fourth person will choose events that will be all about love and connection, and relationships with people.

Now, in any life you have enough material to describe any sort of a life. If you look back into your own life and say; 'let me find all the events of joy' you will find a lot of them. If you say; 'let me find all the events of terror' or 'let me find all the events of pleasure' you will find that too. If you say you want to find all the events of loss and pain, you will find that too. This means that when we think of our lives we operate an editing principal that lifts some events into higher relief than others.

It makes certain things stand out and others recede into the background. The things that we cause to stand out are the things which we consider the significant events, those that have formed us.

If you think that you are a person who has been dealt a rough hand by life and that life has been so awful to you, you will feel that you are now in a place where you have no control over your life. When you look back at your life the events that you will pick out, will all be events that confirm that picture of not having any control and of being broken or of being lost.

Another person may think of themselves as a cheerful person. This person is always the soul of the party and who is loved by others. When that person looks back on his life what he will find is mainly the events of love. This means that every life has enough material to make for any kind of story. It is the particular events you choose to make significant that together construct your biography, your idea of who you are. You cannot tell the whole story because then you will have to relive it. So obviously there is an editing mechanism in action. If you were to recount everything that has happened to you from the moment you were born you will need a life as long as the life you have had to recount every moment. So you have to edit. Now when you start editing you choose some events over others.

Why is it that you choose these events? It is because you have a view of who you are. In other words when you look back in your biography, your biography is such a big thing that by definition you edit it. Your biography does not create you, you create your biography. You create your biography based on your assumption of who you are, of what you are and of what the issues are in your life right now.

That gives you a taste of the extraordinary power that we as human beings have. We are not defined, at every turn we are the actual definers. Our past does not tell us who we are, we tell our past what it is. You can choose moment by moment to change. You can choose right now to say; 'You know what? My life has been a wonderful life.', and you will find all the events of wonder. You can say; 'You know what? My life has been an adventurous life.' And you will find the events of adventure. You can say; 'You know what? My life has been an ecstatic life.' Likewise if you look back at it you will find moments of ecstasy. So why do you settle for a miserable picture? Why do you settle for a depressed picture?

We limit ourselves. We limit our capacity to experience our true nature. We sentence ourselves to misery. We sentence ourselves to feeling incomplete and lost. This sentence is based on us clinging to a notion that we somehow need to get something out there which is not where we are now to make us happy. 'I have got to marry, I have got to have a wife, I have got to get this job, and I have got to get that amount of money' or 'Oh, if only I had this or if only I had that'.

In the process you sentence yourself to a sense of limitation and of misery. This limitation of misery is based on assumptions that you have developed in your past about what it means to be happy. For example, 'since I was 4 years old I wanted to drive a train. Well, I have never driven a train. Now what an unfortunate and unhappy man I am.

Now I am going to throw myself into the Klip River and drown myself because I have not driven a train'. The worst thing that can happen to me is for somebody to actually let me drive a train because I will discover the most staggering anti-climax of my life.

If I look back at my life with wisdom I start to see this desire that I got so fascinated with as a 4 year old cannot be a sensible criterion on which I build my contentment. We sentence ourselves to being miserable, we sentence ourselves to being unhappy, we sentence ourselves to being discontented. Our suffering is based on what we have chosen to make significant.**58**

You cannot choose the world that you are in, but you can choose your response to that world. In the words of the famous Crosby, Stills, Nash and Young song, *"If you can't be with the one you love, love the one you're with."* If the things you are looking at in the world make you unhappy, look at other things. If what you are getting from life makes you unhappy, look at what you are contribut ing. You have no power over what comes to you. You have absolute power over what leaves you.

We must understand that while we are miserable and un- happy we cannot do what Allah has called on us to do. He has only made us to worship Him. Worshipping Him means being amazed; being like a little child that has seen something wonderful. You cannot be like a little child that has seen something wonderful if you are depressed and miserable. By looking at those things which make you unhappy you become even more unhappy. When you are miserable about the world you cannot see that it is wonderful.

Being miserable means that the world you are in does not fill you with wonder. You are therefore not worshipping. You are not doing with your life what it has been designed to do. When you do not apply something to its purpose you break it. I live in a house where all our knives have twisted tips, because our sons keep on using them as screw drivers. When you do not apply a thing to its purpose you break it.

This means that being unhappy sentences you to more unhappiness. You cannot do your job of being enawed and in worship if you are not fundamentally happy.

May Allah grant us peaceful hearts. May Allah grant us happiness.
May Allah grant us joy.
May Allah grant us going on by Him. May Allah grant us the garden.
May Allah grant us the highest.

Al Hamdulillah.

————

58: F.A. - *"Our deepest fear is not that we are inadequate. Our deepest fear is that we are powerful beyond measure. It is our light not our darkness that most frightens us."* Marianne Williamson

You contain all of Existence!
Discourse 28: Undated

Bismillahir Rahmanir Rahim:

We are an interspace between two realms of existence. There is that which is in front of us, that is the world of phenomenal existence and tangible things, and there is that which is behind us, behind our eyes in the depths of our inner beings. The way things have been set up is that these two realms are mirrors of each other and in so far as they are mirrors of each other they are also inverted images of each other. They reflect opposites of each other and in that reflection discover their true natures.

If we look at the world in the way we normally look at it, it presents itself as big, as infinite. Stretching in front of you and behind you, on top of you and below you is the rest of existence and it appears to be very large, it appears to wrap around you. It appears that you are in the middle of the world that you exist in. You are in that sense epi-central to being. You are in the centre of existence.

Consciousness has been set up in such a way that, at first glance, the world will always present itself to you as all around you, and this phenomenon will, by definition, place you in the centre. This world that encapsulates you and wraps around you presents itself as being vast, majestic, enormous, immeasurable and infinite.

At the same time our usual experience of what is behind our eyes; of our inner lives is that it is a place of limitations; a small place. It is a place of your privacy, which by definition is surround- ed by that which is vast. This is how things appear to be. The other is vast and you are tiny. The other is majestic and you are small in the face of that other.

This is not the truth of the matter. The truth of the matter is that although you experience yourself as small there are in fact no limitations to your inner space. If you allow yourself to become quiet, allow yourself to sink into the moment that you are in, and allow yourself to experience what is behind your eyes, you will discover that it has no back. There is no back to your being. This back that you are trying to stretch into also has no bottom and it has no top, and it does not have sides. Your body almost presents itself in front of this nothingness, this vastness, and this vastness has no dimension, it is not measurable. It is truly infinite.

So the world presents itself in such a way that the other, the outward, the seen, appears infinite and that the self, the seer, appears finite. In fact it is exactly the other way around because when you think about the other as limitless space, it is by definition an unending measure of limitations. We say that one cannot imagine travelling in one direction and never coming to the end because there cannot be an end. Every kilometre that you travel will reveal another kilometre to travel. If you say that you are surrounded by infinite space it means that stretching from you in every direction is an infinite number of kilometres. This is like saying an immeasurable number of measures. In other words it is infinity by metaphor, by metaphor of measurement. Immeasurable measurability is a kind of paradox. It is a metaphor to give us a feel of infinity. It is infinity by the metaphor of finiteness.

However, this emptiness that is at the back of your being, that which constitutes your inward, is not measurable, there are no kilometres to it. When you are at the middle of it, you are at the edge of it. Where is the end of it? It has no beginning and it has no end.

This means that it is your nature to have access to that which is truly infinite and which has absolutely no sides and no bottom to it. It is the whole universe in a spot, and that happens to be the spot that constitutes the totality of you being. This means to say that the infinity that you have access to behind your eyes is the real infinity. The infinity that you see and apprehend in front of your eyes is infinite limitation. The outer is metaphorical infinity, the inner is real infinity. We think of the inner as the realm of metaphor and the outer the realm of things as they are. The reality is precisely the other way around.

In other words we learn to view our inner life to be a life of limitation and the outer world, the ardh, to be a place of freedom, it is limitation. It is your inner life, your inner being which is limitless. This means that as we mature in our inner life we start to get tastes of a state which makes everything else almost silly, almost like a puppet show. The outer stops having the gravity and realness that it usually has because you start to understand that the real existence is within.

We get brought up to think that we are defined by the world that we are in, but this is not so. We define the world that we are in. It does not define us, we define it. This idea that as you stand here existence wraps around you is only true in a hypothetical sense, because you have to imagine yourself being surrounded by the rest of existence.

How you actually experience existence if you stop and look for long enough is that it does not wrap itself around you, because whatever it is that you experience you will notice you are experiencing it as being in front of you. It is almost as if the reflector, the mirror which sees all this stuff, is behind all your experience and your experience comes at it from the front. Even one's hearing works like that. Although when you hear something it is almost as if it crawls around you and then registers in the front of your being, the front of your awareness. Your awareness is directed at it, so you see it.

Use your eyesight for example. Whatever you see presents itself in front of you. If you explore the limits of the picture that you see, if you give attention to the circle at the limit of your peripheral vision, you will notice that anything that you see will always be contained within that circle, that boundary. The seen or outer is contained within and in front of the boundary at the limit of your peripheral vision and the seer or inward is behind that boundary and outside of that boundary. The seen is limited by boundary and contained by boundary while the seer is outside boundary and contains boundary. The seen is limited and the seer is unlimited.

If you now allow the place that your attention is func- tioning from to sink a little deeper into the emptiness behind the boundary, in other words, if you allow yourself to sink deeper into yourself, then you discover that the other presents itself to you in a sphere.

When you take your attention to the bottom of that sphere you discover the same emptiness that you find behind or on top of that sphere. If you allow your attention to function from a deep enough place, the seer almost slips around the sides.

Once you discover that you are not in the world but the world is in you, you wrap around existence. Existence does not wrap around you. This is the significance of the account of Allah saying that the entire universe cannot contain Him, but that the heart of the 'mu'min' can contain Him. This is not a metaphor, this is how it actually works. The whole of existence is inside of you.

If you try and discover the edges of your being and you work on the edges you think are there you will discover that your being has no edges. It has no back and it has no sides. Everything that you experience presents itself to you in a sphere. We can refer to this as the bubble of perception. Everything that you perceive is in a bubble and it is almost as if you are looking into a bubble from the outside. When you move your head the bubble moves, and everything you perceive stays in the bubble. You are outside the bubble and the bubble is inside you. The world does not contain you, you contain the world. How things appear is the exact opposite of how they are.

When you see things as they are you will discover that the bubble is inside you. This means that when you look at the furthest horizon you see yourself on the other side of that horizon. You wrap around existence.

So while we view ourselves in the middle of existence, while we look at life from the point of view that we are tiny and that the world defines and encapsulates us, we are in the tyrannical hold of an illusion. Then all we have is our perception of limitations. What you must understand is that your perception of limita tion is a 'program'; it is not what is actually going on.

As you progress on this journey you start experiencing states where you really have this perception (that you are not in the world but that the world is in you). That state eventually becomes a station (i.e. it becomes more or less permanent). Until you have tasted that station, you have not achieved the fullness of your life. You have not achieved the highest possibility.

Everything that we do until we achieve this possibility is like a very poor black and white photograph next to the Technicolour possibility of this way of existence. If we see with the Technicolour perspective we become truly unconditional beings because we are no longer imposed on by the world. This is the journey that we are on. This is the journey of escape. This is the journey of freedom.

You are taught the terror that the world is on top of you and wraps around you, and that you are in its clutches. Based on this illusion you are a prisoner of existence, and of your limitations, in a station of being lost. But then, with practice and following the path, you discover that you are not contained by the universe but that you contain it. This is arrival. This is being found. How can that which was not lost be found? Our blessing from our Rabb is that we are in exile so that we can savour the sweetness of home coming.

May Allah grant us success on the path.
May Allah grant us nearness to Him.
May Allah grant us annihilation in Him.
May Allah grant us death before we die.
May Allah bless our beloved Prophet Muhammad, and his family and his companions and the transmitters who have carried his heart to us over the centuries.

Al Hamdulillah.

Revolution of the Self:
Discourse 30: Undated

Bismillahir Rahmanir Rahim:

In the Qur'an Allah presents us with the account of the events around the journey of Bilqis or the queen of Sheba to Sayyidina Suleiman (a.s.). The visit was prompted when the Prophet Suleiman (a.s.) sent an embassy to the queen calling on her to accept the Oneness of Allah. She then took council with her chiefs asking them what to do and she said; 'We must be careful because we do notwant this man here' She said that when a king comes to a city he only comesto despoil it and to debase its nobility.

Shaykh Fadhlallah has used this account of the queen's description of the despoiling of the city and the debasement of the nobility as a metaphor for the path. He says the nafs is like a city. This is true. Within you, within your character you have the high and the low, you have the Northern and the Southern Suburbs, you have the poor and you have the rich. Your being is vast; your being is like a city.

When the king comes to visit He will leave it a place of ruin because a king cannot come to a city but to despoil it. This was the practice of the kings of old. In the city of Lincoln in England there was a visit by one of the kings in the Twelfth Century and to this day they can still tell you what it cost the city. It is still on record. How many cattle that were slaughtered and how much wheat had to be sold. The visit of the king for a couple of weeks impoverished the city. When the king visits a city the citizens are left bereft.

So it is with us. We think that we are in charge. We think that we have the affair under our thumb. We think that we can manage our own lives. Understand that when we open ourselves to the highest possibility to be occupiedby the Malik of all creation, thereis no place for ourselves any more. The event causes an overturning of what you thought was important and significant.

All of us have the equivalent of nobility inside of ourselves. We have that which we consider to be significant like the nobles of the city; the ones who have the privilege; the ones who are in charge; the ones who govern the affair. We all have the equivalent of that inside ourselves.

This one says that the nobility in his life is his Beloved. The second one has made his nobility his wealth, his significance and his popularity. The third one has made his nobility his pursuit of knowledge. The fourth one has made the nobility of his life how many women he can bed. We all make things significant in our lives.

Understand that when the King comes to visit all of that is under threat, what you have is literally an inversion of the state of affairs. Further, in the same account Allah indicates that those who were oppressed before would become those who will be raised to a higher station, and those who were in high stations will be pushed under.

The things which we try to avoid, and to which we generally do not grant significance in our lives; may be those qualities of obedience, humbleness, generosity, gratitude and trust. Those things that almost turn us into simpletons and fools are the things to which we generally do not grant significance. With the visitation of the King those are the qualities that get raised into eminence and pre-eminence. The other qualities we have which we build our lives around will become debased.

This matter is about an overturning. It is a revolution of the self. It is an overturning of priorities. Tawheda reminded me the other day about this famous rule of thumb in our tradition that says you will not achieve the highest if you do not sweep the ash heaps of the world with yourself. If you do not know how to make yourself thoroughly insignificant you cannot achieve the highest.

The secret of making yourself insignificant is really one of understanding how the self has been designed. Like nobility we want to make ourselves very important and very significant.

However, we do not understand that our strength does not lie in being seen to be significant. Our strength lies in our capacity to grant significance.

If you want to be important to somebody else that person can withhold from you this thing that you want from him. Because they can withhold it they have power over you. Then they become significant and you become weak.

We are not here to claim - we are here to grant. Consider where the real power lies. Does it lie with the one who gives significance, or with the one who is given significance? When you start making the other important, when you start granting significance to the otherthen by implication ignore it for yourself, you have become the criterion whereby the other is measured. You become the witness. You have become the centre. Who is more powerful, the king or the king maker? Where does the real authority lie, with the one who grants significance or the one who claims significance?

If you want to be seen to be important you get pushed to the side. Then you are not in the middle, you are peripheral. The reason why you are peripheral is because you put power over you in the hands of the other. The moment you change the discourse and say: 'I do not want anything from you, so you cannot withhold from me, you do not have power over me, I am not going to grant it to you', then you move from the side to the middle.

This status of being in the middle is what you have been designed to be and this status is exactly what ihsaan is all about. You see our current worldviewis based on a particular kind of self, and that is the objective observer. In other words the observer is outside of the drama. Now that is not possible because we know that as soon as you observe, by the fact of observing you have changed the matter. **62**

When you act as a person among others you are not on the side, you are in the middle of the matter. You are not the insignificant one who is peripheral to the affair; you are the granter of significance who is in the middle of the affair. With the observer, what happens is that your witnessing is only a small reflection of the witnessing that is actually going on. We know that the definition of ihsaan is that you worship Allah in such a way that you know He sees you even if you do not see Him.

In otherwords the One Seer that sees all is observing you from 360 degrees around you, like a sphere of observation. From every single angle, what is hidden, what is manifest, what is silent, what is spoken, what is on the left, what is on the right, what is on top, what is at the bottom, it is all witnessed. This means that when you start granting significance then you become that which is truly witnessed. You move into the middle of the affair. You start becoming aware that you are being watched. There is a journey involved. The journey initially looks like madness because it is about a complete despoiling of what we think is normally important. The despoiling makes a particular shift possible. There are two ways of measuring a person and the significance of a person. One is to measure the significance of the person's life on a basis of facts and actions. This one has built that tower, that one has conquered an army, that one has built a bridge. These things are concerned with things that we do. These things are the active side; the side of 'ardh,of amilu salihaat. Now that is all wonderful but that is only one side of the matter. The other side of the matter is aminu; belief.

Belief is an inner event that affects perception. Everything that we do is in the realm of ruin. There is nothing that you will do that will have any permanence. The most important thing that you do will probably not be remembered ten years after your death. Everything that you do is in the realm of despoiling, of being ravished.

Changing how you perceive is about encapsulating the entire universe. Allah says; 'The entire universe cannot contain Him but the heart of the mu'min contains Him'. In other words within your perception it is possible to contain the whole universe. The most significant thing that you can do is not to achieve great feats in the world. It is about achieving feats of perception. **63** Changing how you view things.

The journey is therefore as follows: We start off by attempting to be significant, which makes us weak and peripheral. The King then comes to visit and despoils our pretentious nobility.

At this point we make the other significant and in so doing we move from the futile attempt to be king to becoming the maker of kings. Suddenly we are not peripheral, but we are the one in the middle who grants all their significance.

Granting significance is about defining what is worthy to be seen. It is about witnessing. The degree to which we truly witness is the degree to which we become witnessed. We begin to experience that the observer looking through our eyes is the One Divine Witness. At this point we are no longer in the middle because we have moved to the periphery. However, this periphery is not a place of being irrelevant and cast aside. It is the place where the Totality of the self encapsulates the other.

May Allah grant us success on the path.
May Allah grant us nearness to Him.
May Allah grant us annihilation in Him.
May Allah grant us death before we die.
Oh Allah, grant peace and blessing on our beloved Messenger, on his family
and on his companions.

Al Hamdulillah.

———

62: T.S. - This is Heisenberg's Uncertainty Principle.
63: T.S. - This usuallydoesn't mean seeingspirits and visionsetc, they belong in the 'Seas of the Essence', not in Reality.

GLOSSARY

Abd:	Literally a slave. The one who is in total submission on the Will of Allah.
Akhira:	The afterlife.
Al Hamdullillah:	"All praise be to Allah"
Allah Subahana wa'ta Allah:	"Allah, Glorious and Most High is He"
Allahu Akbar:	Allah is the most great.
Amilus-salihaat:	Doing good works
Aql:	The intellect or the faculty of reason.
Ar Rahmanir Rahim	The Most Compassionate, The Most Merciful.
Ardh:	The Earth.
A.S.:	Alaihis-Salam "Peace be upon him/her."
Asalaamu Alaykum:	"Peace be upon you."
Astaghfirrullah:	"O Allah, cover me, forgive me."
Badr:	Plain outside of Medina, site of a great battle in the early days of Islam. The battle was a great victory for the early Muslims.
Barakat:	Subtle spiritual energy that flows through everything, but is strongest within the human.
Billah:	In Allah.
Bismillahir Rahmanir Rahim:	In the Name of Allah, the Most Compassionate, the Most Merciful
Dars:	Spiritual teaching, lesson
Deen:	The "life transaction" between Allah and man.
Dhikr:	Remembrance, invocation, or glorification of Allah.

Diwan:	The dynamic and living poetry of great lovers of Allah. The meanings and the effect of the meanings of the diwan are geared to achieve a profound inward change in the perception and subtle awareness of the subject.
Faqir:	The one who is poor and needy towards Allah, knowing his own insignificance in the face of the Majestic, All Significant.
Fardh:	Obligatory.
Fiqh:	Islamic Law.
Fisabilillah:	In the way of Allah. Performing an action purely for the pleasure of Allah, as an act of devotion and worship.
Fuqara:	The indigents or the poor and needy ones. The term refers specifically to the spiritual travellers on the Sufi Path. Plural of faqir.
Khalwa:	Spiritual retreat, seclusion, withdrawal. An isolated place where one endeavours to still the mind, silence internal dialogue, and focus attention deep within.
Hadith	A saying of Prophet Muhammad (s.a.w.s.)
Hadith al Qudsi	Words of Allah spoken through the mouth of Prophet Muhammad. A seperate type of Revilation to that of the Qur'an.
Hadra:	Literally means Presence. It also refers to the ritual dance performed in the Shadhili Sufi order.
Halaal:	That which is lawful according to Islamic Law.
Haqq:	Deep truth of reality.
Harraam:	That which is forbidden according Islamic Law.

Hashunallah wa ni'mal al Wakil:	"Allah is sufficient for me and He is the Best of Protectors."
Himma:	Intense spiritual resolve or yearning. The sincere and dedicated application of one's efforts and strivings toward attaining the desired object.
Houri's:	The beautiful companions of Paradise, referred to in Qur'an.
Ibada:	Worship and service of Allah with absolute obedience and love.
Ihsaan:	Excellence, sanctifying virtue, perfection, spiritual beauty.
Imaan;	Belief or faith. Imaan is also to feel secure and safe in that belief.
Innamal 'amalu bin niyyati:	All actions are judged by their intentions.
Insha' Allah:	Allah willing,.
Iqraa:	Literally "Read" or "Recite". The first word of Divine Revelation to the Prophet Muhammad. (s.a.w.s.)
Islam:	Submission or surrender.
Istighfaar:	Seeking to be covered by Allah, seeking His forgiveness.
Jehannam:	Hell
Jalsa:	Sitting. The term refers particularly to the fifth posture of prayer (salah).
Jannat:	Paradise. The Garden.
Jihad:	Lit: struggle. The constant and vigilant inner struggle against the nafs or lower self.
Kafir:	One who covers the Truth, an unbeliever.
Kalimah:	The Islamic testimony of Faith: "There is no god, only Allah. Muhammad is the Messenger of Allah."
Khalif:	A viceregent of Allah.

Kufr:	Covering up or denial or suppression of the Truth.
La illaha il Allah:	There is no god only The God (Allah).
Majdhoob:	The one who is under the influence of Divine Attraction. The power of the Attraction brings about spiritual intoxication and indifference to all that is other-than-Allah.
Malik:	King.
Malik al Mout:	Angel of death, lit: King of death
Masha' Allah:	As Allah Willed.
Mimbar:	The pulpit from which the Imam gives his sermon at Friday prayers.
Mu'min:	The believer or the one with faith.
Muqaddam:	The one who goes before. Designated representative of the Shaykh.
Murabit:	A member of the Murabitun movement.
Murabitun:	Movement led by Shaykh Abdul Qadir as-Sufi.
Mureed:	The one who desires Allah. The seeker of Reality.
Murshid:	The spiritual teacher or guide.
Musallah:	The prayer carpet.
Muslim:	The one who has submitted and surrendered to Allah.
Nabi:	A prophet.
Nabi Issa:	The Prophet Jesus (a.s.)
Nafs:	The self or ego.
Niyyah:	Intention.
Qasida:	Poem or ode.
Rabb:	The Lord.
Rahmat:	Mercy.

Ramadan:	The Islamic month of fasting.
Rasullulah:	The Messenger of Allah, the Prophet Muhammad (s.a.w.s.)
Ruh:	Soul or Spirit.
Safa and Marwa	Two hillocks in Mecca between which, according to al-Qur'an, Bibi Hagar ran in search of water for her baby Ismael (A.S.)
Sajda:	Prostration.
Salah:	Islamic ritual prayer.
(s.a.w.s.) Sallallahu Aleihi wa sallam:	These words are spoken after the hearing or reading the name of the Prophet Muhammad. Literally, "May the Blessings of Allah be upon him and Peace."
Shahada:	The witnessing. The Islamic testimony of Faith: "I bear witness that there is no god, but Allah. I bear witness that Muhammad is the Messenger of Allah."
Shahid:	The witness.
Shariah:	The Islamic Sacred Law.
Shaykh:	Literally, "old man", but in this context, the Sufi master or teacher.
Shirk:	Idolatry, to worship that which is other-than-Allah.
Shukran:	Thank you, in Arabic.
Subhaanallah:	"Glory be to Allah."
Subhaana wa' ta Allah:	"Glorious and Most High is Allah."
Sunnah:	The way of the Prophet Muhammad (s.a.w.s.).
Surah:	The form, outer form of an entity or thing, concealing the inner meaning. It also means a chapter of the Qur'an.
Takbir:	Pronouncing the words "Allahu Akbar" at the beginning of ritual prayer.
Taqdir:	Fate or destiny.

Taqwa:	Being conscious of Allah, God conciousness. Awe of Allah.
Tasawwuf:	Sufism, the inner dimension of Islam.
Tauba:	Turning towards Allah.
Thawab:	Reward, in the afterlife.
Ummah:	The past and present community of the Prophet Muhammad (s.a.w.s.).
Wahhabi:	A follower of the doctrine of Muhammad Ibn Abdal Wahhab. The name can designate an extreme Islamic fundamentalist.
Wahm:	Illusion.
Waqt:	Time, the moment, now.
Wird:	A specific spiritual exercise comprisedof various litanies and Divine Names.
Zahid:	An ascetic or one who renounces the world.
Zakat:	The Islamic tax.
Zawia:	Literally means "a corner". A place designated for the transmission of the Sufic teaching from the Master to his mureed's. Originally, the teaching took place under a tree and later developed into a specific room, then a building and then a complex of buildings.

About the Author

Etsko Schuitema is a renowned business consultant who has authored numerous books including 'Leadership' and 'The Millenium Discourses'. He is a senior partner in Schuitema, a transformational consultancy operating worldwide. Etsko is also a Shaykh or teacher in the Shadhili-Darqawi Sufi tradition and is known as Shaykh Ebrahim.

OTHER BOOKS BY THE AUTHOR